Songs of a Semite

by

Emma Lazarus

LITERATURE HOUSE / GREGG PRESS
Upper Saddle River, N. J.

Republished in 1970 by
LITERATURE HOUSE
an imprint of The Gregg Press
121 Pleasant Avenue
Upper Saddle River, N. J. 07458

Standard Book Number—8398-11535
Library of Congress Card—70-104509

Printed in United States of America

Songs of a Semite.

THE DANCE TO DEATH,

AND OTHER POEMS,

— BY —

818.
4
LAZ

EMMA LAZARUS,

AUTHOR OF "ADMETUS, AND OTHER POEMS," "ALIDE," "TRANSLATIONS
FROM HEINE," ETC.

———

NEW YORK :
OFFICE OF "THE AMERICAN HEBREW,"
498-500 THIRD AVENUE.
1882.

CONTENTS.

The Dance to Death;

A HISTORICAL TRAGEDY

IN FIVE ACTS,

— BY —

EMMA LAZARUS.

NEW YORK:
"THE AMERICAN HEBREW" PUBLISHING COMPANY,
498-500 THIRD AVENUE.
1882.

PHIL. COWEN, PRINTER,
498–500 THIRD AVE., N. Y.

THIS PLAY IS DEDICATED,

IN PROFOUND VENERATION AND RESPECT

TO THE MEMORY OF

GEORGE ELIOT,

THE ILLUSTRIOUS WRITER,

WHO DID MOST AMONG THE ARTISTS OF OUR DAY

TOWARDS ELEVATING AND ENNOBLING

THE SPIRIT OF JEWISH NATIONALITY.

THE PERSONS.

FREDERICK THE GRAVE—Landgrave of Thuringia and Margrave of Meissen, Protector and Patron of the Free City of Nordhausen.

PRINCE WILLIAM OF MEISSEN—His Son.

SÜSSKIND VON ORB—A Jew.

HENRY SCHNETZEN—Governor of Salza.

HENRY NORDMANN OF NORDMANNSTEIN—Knight of Treffurt.

REINHARD PEPPERCORN—Prior of Wartburg Monastery.

RABBI JACOB.

DIETRICH VON TETTENBORN—President of the Council.

REUBEN VON ORB—a boy, Süsskind's son.

BARUCH,
NAPHTALI, } Jews.

RABBI CRESSELIN.

LAY BROTHER.

PAGE.

PUBLIC SCRIVENER.

PRINCESS MATHILDIS: Wife to Frederick.

LIEBHAID VON ORB.

CLAIRE CRESSELIN.

Jews, Jewesses, Burghers, Senators, Flagellants, Servants, Guardsmen.

———

SCENE:—Partly in Nordhausen, partly in Eisenach.
TIME:—May 4th, 5th, 6th, 1349.

THE DANCE TO DEATH.

ACT I.—*In Nordhausen.*

SCENE I. A Street in the Judengasse, outside the Synagogue. During this scene Jews and Jewesses, singly and in groups, with prayer-books in their hands pass across the stage and go into the Synagogue. Among them, enter BARUCH and NAPHTALI.

NAPHTALI.   Hast seen him yet?
BARUCH.   Nay, Rabbi Jacob's door
Swung to behind him, just as I puffed up
O'erblown with haste. See how our years weigh, cousin.
Who'd judge me with this paunch a temperate man,
A man of modest means, a man withal
Scarce overpast his prime?   Well, God be praised,
If age bring no worse burden! Who is this stranger?
Simon the Leech tells me he claims to bear
Some·special message from the Lord—no doubt
To-morrow, fresh from rest, he'll publish it
Within the Synagogue
NAPHTALI.   To-morrow, man?
He will not hear of rest—he comes anon—
Shall we within?
BARUCH.   Rather let's wait,
And scrutinize him as he mounts the street.
Since you denote him so remarkable,
You've whetted my desire.
NAPHTALI.   A blind, old man,
Mayhap is all you'll find him—spent with travel,
His raiment fouled with dust, his sandaled feet
Road-bruised by stone and bramble. But his face!—
Majestic with long fall of cloud-white beard,
And hoary wreath of hair—oh, it is one
Already kissed by angels,
BARUCH.   Look, there limps
Little Manasseh, bloated as his purse,
And wrinkled as a frost-pinched fruit. I hear
His last loan to the Syndic will result
In quadrupling his wealth. Good Lord! what luck
Blesses some folk, while good men stint and sweat
And scrape, to merely fill the household larder.
What said you of this pilgrim, Naphtali?

These inequalities of fortune rub
My sense of justice so against the grain,
I ose my very name.   Whence does he come?
Is he alone?
    NAPHTALI,   He comes from Chinon, France,
Rabbi Cresselin he calls himself—alone
Save for his daughter who has led him hither.
A beautiful, pale girl with round black eyes.
    BARUCH.   Bring they fresh tidings of the pestilence?
    NAPHTALI   I know not—but I learn from other source
It has burst forth at Erfurt.
    BARUCH.   God have mercy!
Have many of our tribe been stricken?
    NAPHTALI.   No
They cleanse their homes and keep their bodies sweet,
Nor cease from prayer—and so does Jacob's God
Protect His chosen, still.   Yet even His favor
Our enemies would twist into a curse.
Beholding the destroying angel smite
The foul idolator and leave unscathed
The gates of Israel—the old cry they raise—
We have begotten the Black Death—*we* poison
The well-springs of the towns.
    BARUCH.   God pity us!
But truly are we blessed in Nordhausen.
Such terrors seem remote as Egypt's plagues.
I warrant you our Landgrave dare not harry
Such creditors as we.   See, here comes one,
The greatest and most liberal of them all—
Süsskind von Orb.

    (SUSSKIND VON ORB, LIEBHAID and REUBEN enter, all pass across the stage, and disappear within the Synagogue.)

                I'd barter my whole fortune,
And yours to boot, that's thrice the bulk of mine,
For half the bonds he holds in Frederick's name.
The richest merchant in Thuringia, he—
The poise of his head would tell it, knew we not.
How has his daughter leaped to womanhood!
I mind when she came toddling by his hand,
But yesterday—a flax-haired child—to-day
Her brow is level with his pompous chin.
    NAPHTALI.   How fair she is!   Her hair has kept its gold
Untarnished still.   I trace not either parent
In her face, clean cut as a gem.
    BARUCH.   Her mother
Was far-off kin to me, and I might pass,
I'm told, unguessed in Christian garb.   I know
A pretty secret of that scornful face.

It lures high game to Nordhausen.

NAPHTALI.   Baruch,
I marvel at your prompt credulity.
The Prince of Meissen and Liebhaid von Orb!
A jest for gossips and—Look, look, he comes!

BARUCH.   Who's that, the Prince?

NAPHTALI.   Nay, dullard, the old man,
The Rabbi of Chinon.   Ah! his stout staff,
And that brave creature's strong young hand suffice
Scarcely to keep erect his tottering frame.
Emaciate-lipped,with cavernous black eyes
Whose inward visions do eclipse the day,
Seems he not one re-risen from the grave
To yield the secret?

(Enter RABBI JACOB, and RABBI CRESSELIN led by CLAIRE. They walk across the stage, and disappear in the Synagogue.)

BARUCH. (*Exaltedly.*)   Blessed art thou, O Lord,
King of the Universe, who teachest wisdom
To those who fear thee!*

NAPHTALI.   Haste we in.   The star
Of Sabbath dawns.

BARUCH.   My flesh is still a-creep
From the strange gaze of those wide-rolling orbs,
Didst note, man, how they fixed me?   His lean cheeks,
As wan as wax, were bloodless; now his arms
Stretched far beyond the flowing sleeve and showed
Gaunt, palsied wrists, and hands blue-tipped with death!
Well, I have seen a sage of Israel.

(They enter the Synagogue.   Scene closes.)

SCENE II.   The Synagogue crowded with worshipers.   Among the women in the Gallery are discovered LIEBHAID VON ORB and CLAIRE CRESSELIN.   Below, among the men, SUSSKIND VON ORB and REUBEN.   At the Reader's Desk, RABBI JACOB.   Fronting the audience under the Ark of the Covenant, stands a high desk, behind which is seen the white head of an old man bowed in prayer.   BARUCH and NAPHTALI enter and take their seats.

BARUCH.   Think you he speaks before the service?

NAPHTALI.   Yea.
Lo, phantom-like the towering patriarch!

(RABBI CRESSELIN slowly rises beneath the Ark.)

RABBI CRESSELIN.   Woe unto Israel! woe unto all
Abiding 'mid strange peoples!   Ye shall be
Cut off from that land where ye made your home.
I, Cresselin of Chinon, have traveled far,
Thence where my fathers dwelt, to warn my race,
For whom the fire and stake have been prepared.
Our brethren of Verdun, all over France,

---

* These words are the customary formula of Jewish prayer on seeing a wise man of Israel.

Are burned alive beneath the *Goyim's* torch.
What terrors have I witnessed, ere my sight
Was mercifully quenched! In Gascony,
In Savoy, Piedmont, round the garden shores
Of tranquil Leman, down the beautiful Rhine,
At Lindau, Costnitz, Schafhausen, St. Gallen,
Everywhere torture, smoking Synagogues,
Carnage and burning flesh.   The lights shine out
Of Jewish virtue, Jewish truth, to star
The sanguine field with an immortal blazon,
The venerable Mar-Isaac in Cologne,
Sat in his house at prayer, nor lifted lid
From off the sacred text, while all around
The fanatics ran riot; him they seized
Haled through the streets, with prod of stick and spike
Fretted his wrinkled flesh, plucked his white beard,
Dragged him with gibes into their Church, and held
A Crucifix before him. " Know thy Lord!"
He spat thereon; he was pulled limb from limb.
I saw— God, that I might forget! —a man
Leap in the Loire, with his fair, stalwart son,
A-bloom with youth, and midst the stream unsheathe
A poniard, sheathing it in his boy's heart,
While he pronounced the blessing for the dead.
" Amen!" the lad responded as he sank,
And the white water darkened as with wine.
I saw—but no! You are glutted, and my tongue
Blistered, refuseth to narrate more woe.
I have known much sorrow.   When it pleased the Lord
To afflict us with the horde of *Pastoureaux*,
The rabble of armed herdsmen peasants, slaves,
Men-beasts of burden— coarse as the earth they tilled,
Who like an inundation deluged France
To drown our race—my heart held firm, my faith
Shook not upon her rock until I saw
Smit by God's beam, the big, black cloud dissolve.
Then followed with their scythes, spades, clubs and banners
Flaunting the Cross, the hosts of Armleder,
From whose fierce wounds we scarce are healed to-day.
Yet do I say the cup of bitterness
That Israel has drained is but a draught
Of cordial to the cup that is prepared.
The Black Death and the Brothers of the Cross,
These are our foes—and these are everywhere.
I who am blind, see ruin in their wake,
Ye who have eyes and limbs, arise and flee!
To-morrow the Flagellants will be here.
God's angel visited my sleep and spake.

" Thy Jewish kin in the Thuringian town
Of Nordhausen, shall be swept off from earth,
Their elders and their babes — consumed with fire.
Go, summon Israel to flight—take this
As sign that I, who call thee, am the Lord,
Thine eyes shalt be struck blind till thou hast spoken."
Then darkness fell upon my mortal sense,
But light broke o'er my soul, and all was clear,
And I have journeyed hither with my child
O'er mount and river, till I have announced
The message of the Everlasting God.

(Sensation in the Synagogue.)

RABBI JACOB   Father, have mercy! when wilt thou have done
With rod and scourge?   Beneath thy children's feet
Earth splits, fire springs.   No rest, no rest, no rest!
A VOICE.   Look to the women! Mariamne swoons!
ANOTHER VOICE.   Woe unto us who sinned!
ANOTHER VOICE.   We're all dead men.
Fly, fly ere dawn as our forefathers fled
From out the land of Egypt.
BARUCH.   Are ye mad?
Shall we desert snug homes? forego the sum
Scraped through laborious years to smooth life's slope,
And die like dogs unkenneled and untombed,
At bidding of a sorrow-crazed old man?
A VOICE.   He flouts the Lord's anointed!   Cast him forth!
SUSSKIND VON ORB.   Peace, brethren, peace! If I have ever served
Israel with purse, arm, brain or heart—now hear me!
May God instruct my speech!   This wise old man,
Whose brow flames with the majesty of truth,
May be part-blinded through excess of light,
As one who eyes too long the naked sun,
Setting in rayless glory, turns and finds
Outlines confused, familiar colors changed,
All objects branded with one blood-bright spot.
Nor chafe at Baruch's homely sense; truth floats
Midway between the stars and the abyss.
We, by God's grace, have found a special nest
I' the dangerous rock, screened against wind and hawk;
Free burghers of a free town, blessed moreover
With the peculiar favor of the Prince,
Frederick the Grave, our patron and protector.
What shall we fear?   Rather, where shall we seek
Secure asylum, if here be not one?
Fly?   Our forefathers had the wilderness,
The sea their gateway, and the fire-cored cloud
Their divine guide.   Us, hedged by ambushed foes,
No frank, free, kindly desert shall receive.

Death crouches on all sides, prepared to leap
Tiger-like on our throats, when first we step
From this safe covert. Everywhere the Plague!
As nigh as Erfurt it has crawled—the towns
Reek with miasma, therank fields of spring,
Rain-saturated, are one beautiful—lie,
Smiling profuse life, and secreting death.
Strange how, unbidden, a trivial memory
Thrusts itself on my mind in this grave hour,
I saw a large white bull urged through the town
To slaughter, by a stripling with a goad,
Whom but one sure stamp of that solid heel,
One toss of those mooned horns, one battering blow
Of that square marble forehead, would have crushed,
As we might crush a worm, yet on he trudged,
Patient, in powerful health to death. At once,
As though o' the sudden stung, he roared aloud,
Beat with fierce hoofs the air, shook desperately
His formidable head, and heifer-swift,
Raced through scared, screaming streets. Well, and the end?
He was the promptlier bound and killed and quartered.
The world belongs to man; dreams the poor brute
Some nook has been apportioned for brute life?
Where shall a man escape men's cruelty?
Where shall God's servant cower from his doom?
Let us bide, brethren—we are in His hand.
    RABBI CRESSELIN. (*Uttering a piercing shriek.*) Ah!
Woe unto Israel! Lo, I see again,
As the Ineffable foretold. I see
A flood of fire that streams towards the town.
Look, the destroying Angel with the sword,
Wherefrom the drops of gall are raining down,
Broad-winged, comes flying towards you. Now he draws
His lightning-glittering blade! With the keen edge
He smiteth Israel—ah!
    (He falls back dead. Confusion in the Synagogue.)
    CLAIRE. (*From the Gallery.*) Father! My father!
Let me go down to him!
    LIEBHAID   Sweet girl, be patient.
This is the House of God, and He hath entered.
Bow we and pray.
    Meanwhile, some of the men surround and raise from the ground the body of
RABBI CRESSELIN. Several voices speaking at once.
    1ST VOICE.   He's doomed.
    2D VOICE.   Dead! Dead!
    3D VOICE.   A judgment!
    4TH VOICE. Make way there! Air! Carry him forth! He's warm!
    3D VOICE. Nay, his heart's stopped—his breath has ceased—quite
        dead.

5TH VOICE. Didst mark a diamond lance flash from the roof?
And strike him 'twixt the eyes?
1ST VOICE.   Our days are numbered.
This is the token.
RABBI JACOB.   Lift the corpse and pray.
Shall we neglect God's due observances,
While He is manifest in miracle?
I saw a blaze seven times more bright than fire,
Crest, halo-wise, the patriarch's white head.
The dazzle stung my burning lids—they closed,
One instant—when they oped the great blank cloud
Had settled on his countenance forever.
* Departed brother, mayest thou find the gates
Of heaven open, see the city of peace,
And meet the ministering angels, glad,
Hastening towards thee! May the High Priest stand
To greet and bless thee! Go thou to the end!
Repose in peace and rise again to life.
No more thy sun sets, neither wanes thy moon.
The Lord shall be thy everlasting light;
Thy days of mourning shall be at an end.
For you, my flock, fear nothing; it is writ
As one his mother comforteth, so I
Will comfort you and in Jerusalem
Ye shall be comforted.   Scene closes.

SCENE III. Evening   A crooked byway in the Judengasse.   Enter PRINCE
WILLIAM.
PRINCE W.   Cursed be these twisted lanes! I have missed the clue
Of the close labyrinth.   Nowhere in sight,
Just when I lack it, a stray gaberdine
To pick me up my thread.   Yet when I haste
Through these blind streets, unwishful to be spied,
Some dozen hawk-eyes peering o'er crook'd beaks
Leer recognition, and obsequious caps
Do kiss the stones to greet my princeship.   Bah!
Strange, midst such refuse sleeps so white a pearl.
At last, here shuffles one. (*Enter a Jew.*)
                    Give you good even!
Sir, can you help me to the nighest way
Unto the merchant's house, Süsskind von Orb?
JEW.   Whence come you knowing not the high brick wall,
Without, blank as my palm, o' the inner side,
Muring a palace?   But—do you wish him well?
He is my friend—we must be wary, wary,
We all have warning—Oh, the terror of it!

---

* From this point to the end of the scene is a literal translation of the Hebrew
burial service.

I have not yet my wits!

PRINCE W.   I am his friend.

Is he in peril?   What's the matter, man?

JEW.   Peril?   His peril is no worse than mine,

But the rich win compassion.   God is just,

And every man of us is doomed.   Alack!

He said it—oh those wild, white eyes!

PRINCE W.   I pray you,

Tell me the way to Süsskind's home.

JEW.   Sweet master,

You look the perfect knight, what can you crave

Of us starved, wretched Jews?   Leave us in peace.

The Judengasse gates will shut anon,

Nor ope till morn again for Jew or Gentile.

PRINCE W.   Here's gold.   I am the Prince of Meissen—speak!

JEW.   Oh pardon!   Let me kiss your mantle's edge.

This way, great sir, I lead you there myself,

If you deign follow one so poor, so humble.

You must show mercy in the name of God,

For verily are we afflicted.   Come.

Hard by is Süsskind's dwelling—as we walk

By your good leave I'll tell what I have seen.

(Exeunt.)

SCENE IV. A luxuriously-furnished apartment in Süsskind von Orb's house. Upon a richly-spread supper table stands the seven-branched silver candlestick of the Sabbath eve.   At the table are seated SUSSKIND VON ORB, LIEBHAID and REUBEN.

SUSSKIND.   Drink, children, drink! and lift your hearts to Him

Who gives us the vine's fruit.   (*They drink.*)

How clear it glows;

Like gold within the golden bowl, like fire

Along our veins, after the work-day week

Rekindling Sabbath-fervor, Sabbath-strength.

Verily God prepares for me a table

In presence of mine enemies!   He anoints

My head with oil, my cup is overflowing.

Praise we His name!   Hast thou, my daughter, served

The needs o' the poor, suddenly-orphaned child?

Naught must she lack beneath my roof.

LIEBHAID.   Yea, father.

She prays and weeps within: she had no heart

For Sabbath meal, but charged me with her thanks—

SUSSKIND.   Thou shalt be mother and sister in one to her.

Speak to her comfortably.

REUBEN.   She has begged

A grace of me I happily can grant.

After our evening-prayer, to lead her back

Unto the synagogue, where sleeps her father,

A light at head and foot, o'erwatched by strangers;

She would hold vigil.

SUSSKIND.　　'Tis a pious wish,
Not to be crossed, befitting Israel's daughter.
Go, Reuben; heavily the moments hang,
While her heart yearns to break beside his corpse.
Receive my blessing. (*He places his hands upon his son's head in benediction. Exit Reuben.*)

　　　　　Henceforth her home is here.
In the event to-night, God's finger points
Visibly out of heaven. A thick cloud
Befogs the future. But just here is light

　　　　　(Enter a servant ushering in Prince William.)

SERVANT. His highness Prince of Meissen. (*Exit.*)
SUSSKIND　　Welcome, Prince!
God bless thy going forth and coming in!
Sit at our table and accept the cup
Of welcome which my daughter fills.

　　　　　(Liebhaid offers him wine.)

PRINCE W. (*drinking.*) To thee! (*All take their seats at the table.*)
I heard disquieting news as I came hither.
The apparition in the Synagogue,
The miracle of the message and the death.
Süsskind von Orb, what think'st thou of these things?

SUSSKIND. I think, sir, we are in the hand of God,
I trust the Prince—your father and my friend.

PRINCE W. Trust no man! flee! I have not come to-night
To little purpose　Your arch enemy
The Governor of Salza, Henry Schnetzen,
Has won my father's ear. Since yestereve
He stops at Eisenach, begging of the Prince
The Jews' destruction.

SUSSKIND. (*calmly.*) Schnetzen is my foe,
I know it, but I know a talisman,
Which at a word transmutes his hate to love.
Liebhaid, my child, look cheerly. What is this?
Harm dare not touch thee; the oppressor's curse,
Melts into blessing at thy sight.

LIEBHAID.　　Not fear
Plucks at my heart-strings, father, though the air
Thickens with portents; 'tis the thought of flight,
But no—I follow thee.

PRINCE W.　　Thou shalt not miss
The value of a hair from thy home-treasures.
All that thou lovest, Liebhaid, goes with thee,
Knowest thou, Süsskind, Schnetzen's cause of hate?

SUSSKIND. Tis rooted in an ancient error, born
During his feud with Landgrave Fritz the Bitten,
Your Highness' grandsire—ten years—twenty—back.

Misled to think I had betrayed his castle,
Who knew the secret tunnel to its courts,
He has nursed a baseless grudge, whereat I smile,
Sure to disarm him by the simple truth.
God grant me strength to utter it.
    PRINCE W.   You fancy
The rancor of a bad heart slow distilled
Through venomed years, so at a breath, dissolves.
O good old man, i' the world, not of the world!
Belike, himself forgets the doubtful core
Of this still-curdling, petrifying ooze.
Truth? why truth glances from the callous mass,
A spear against a rock. He hugs his hate,
His bed-fellow, his daily, life-long comrade;
Think you he has slept, ate, drank with it this while,
Now to forego revenge on such slight cause
As the revealed truth?
    SUSSKIND.   You mistake my thought,
Great-hearted Prince, and justly—for I speak
In riddles, till God's time to make all clear.
When His day dawns, the blind shall see.
    PRINCE W.   Forgive me,
If I, in wit and virtue your disciple,
Seem to instruct my master. Accident
Lifts me where I survey a broader field
Than wise men stationed lower. I spy peril,
Fierce flame invisible from the lesser peaks.
God's time is now. Delayed truth leaves a lie
Triumphant. If you harbor any secret,
Potent to force an ear that's locked to mercy,
In God's name, now disbosom it.
    SUSSKIND.   Kind heaven!
Would that my people's safety were assured
So is my child's! Where shall we turn? Where flee?
For all around us the Black Angel broods.
We step into the open jaws of death
If we go hence.
    PRINCE W.   Better to fall beneath
The hand of God, than be cut off by man.
    SUSSKIND.   We are trapped, the springe is set. Not ignorantly
I offered counsel in the synagogue,
Quelled panic with authoritative calm,
But knowing, having weighed the opposing risks.
Our friends in Strasburg have been overmastered,
The imperial voice is drowned, the papal arm
Drops paralyzed—both, lifted for the truth;
We can but front with brave eyes, brow erect,
As is our wont, the fulness of our doom.

PRINCE W.   Then Meissen's sword champions your desperate cause.
I take my stand here where my heart is fixed.
I love your daughter—if her love consent,
I pray you, give me her to wife.
    LIEBHAID.   Ah!
    SUSSKIND.   Prince,
Let not this Saxon skin, this hair's gold fleece,
These Rhine-blue eyes mislead thee—she is alien.
To the heart's core a Jewess—prop of my house,
Soul of my soul—and I? a despised Jew.
    PRINCE W.   Thy propped house crumbles; let my arm sustain
Its tottering base—thy light is on the wane
Let me re-lume it.   Give thy star to me,
Or ever pitch-black night engulf us all—
Lend me your voice, Liebhaid, entreat for me.
Shall this prayer be your first that he denies?
    LIEBHAID.   Father, my heart's desire is one with his.
    SUSSKIND.   Is this the will of God?   Amen!   My children,
Be patient with me, I am full of trouble.
For you, heroic Prince, could aught enhance
Your love's incomparable nobility,
'Twere the foreboding horror of this hour,
Wherein you dare flash forth its lightning-sword.
You reckon not, in the hot, splendid moment
Of great resolve, the cold insidious breath
Wherewith the outer world shall blast and freeze—
But hark!   I own a mystic amulet,
Which you delivering to your gracious father,
Shall calm his rage withal, and change his scorn
Of the Jew's daughter, into pure affection.
I will go fetch it—though I drain my heart
Of its red blood, to yield this sacrifice.

(Exit Süsskind.)

    PRINCE W.   Have you no smile to welcome love with, Liebhaid?
Why should you tremble?
    LIEBHAID.   Prince, I am afraid!
Afraid of my own heart, my unfathomed joy,
A blasphemy against my father's grief,
My people's agony.   I dare be happy—
So happy! in the instant's lull betwixt
The dazzle and the crash of doom.
    PRINCE W.   You read
The omen falsely; rather is your joy
The thrilling harbinger of general dawn.
Did you not tell me scarce a month agone.
When I chanced in on you at feast and prayer,

The holy time's bright legend? of the queen,
Strong, beautiful, resolute, who denied her race
To save her race, who cast upon the die
Of her divine and simple loveliness,
Her life, her soul,—and so redeemed her tribe.
You are my Esther—but I, no second tyrant,
Worship whom you adore, love whom you love!
    LIEBHAID. If I must die with morn, I thank my God.
And thee, my king, that I have lived this night.

           (Enter Süsskind carrying a jeweled casket.)

    SUSSKIND. Here is the chest, sealed with my signet-ring,
A mystery and a treasure lies within,
Whose worth is faintly symboled by these gems,
Starring the case. Deliver it unopened,
Unto the Landgrave. Now, sweet Prince, goodnight.
Else will the Judengasse gates be closed.
    PRINCE W. Thanks, father, thanks. Liebhaid, my
      bride, goodnight.

(He kisses her brow. Süsskind places his hands on the heads of Liebhaid and Prince William.)

    SUSSKIND. Blessed, Oh Lord, art thou, who bringest joy
To bride and bridegroom. Let us thank the Lord.

           (Curtain falls.)

           END OF ACT I.

ACT II.—*At Eisenach.*

SCENE I. A Room in the Landgrave's Palace. FREDERICK THE GRAVE and HENRY
   SCHNETZEN.

    LANDGRAVE. Who tells thee of my son's love for the Jewess?
    SCHNETZEN. Who tells me? Ask the Judengasse walls,
The garrulous stones publish Prince William's visits
To his fair mistress.
    LANDGRAVE. Mistress? ah, such sins
The Provost of St. George's will remit
For half a pound of coppers.
    SCHNETZEN. Think it not!
No light amour this, leaving shield unflecked;
He woos the Jewish damsel as a knight
The lady of his heart.
    LANDGRAVE. Impossible!
    SCHNETZEN. Things more impossible have chanced. Remember
Count Gleichen, doubly wived, who pined in Egypt,
There wed the Pasha's daughter Malachsala,
Nor blushed to bring his heathen paramour

Home to his noble wife Angelica,
Countess of Orlamund. Yea, and the Pope
Sanctioned the filthy sin.
    LANDGRAVE. Himself shall say it.
Ho, Gunther! (*Enter a lackey.*) Bid the Prince of Meissen here.

    (Exit Lackey. The Landgrave paces the stage in agitation. Enter Prince Wililam.)

    PRINCE W. Father, you called me?
    LANDGRAVE. Ay, when were you last
In Nordhausen?
    PRINCE W. This morning I rode hence.
    LANDGRAVE. Were you at Süsskind's house?
    PRINCE W. I was, my liege.
    LANDGRAVE. I hear you entertain unseemly love
For the Jew's daughter,
    PRINCE W. Who has told thee this?
    SCHNETZEN. This I have told him.
    PRINCE W. Father, believe him not.
I swear by heaven 'tis no unseemly love
Leads me to Süsskind's house,
    LANDGRAVE. With what high title
Please you to qualify it?
    PRINCE W. True, I love
Liebhaid von Orb, but 'tis the honest passion
Wherewith a knight leads home his equal wife,
    LANDGRAVE. Great God! and thou wilt brag thy shame! Thou
            speakest
Of wife and Jewess in one breath! Wilt make
Thy princely name a stench in German nostrils?
    PRINCE W. Hold, father, hold! You know her—yes, a Jewess
In her domestic piety, her soul
Large, simple, splendid like a star, her heart
Suffused with Syrian sunshine—but no more—
The aspect of a Princess of Thuringia,
Swan-necked, gold-haired, Madonna-eyed. I love her!
If you will quench this passion, take my life!
    (He falls at his father's feet. Frederick, in a paroxysm of rage, seizes his sword.)
    SCHNETZEN. He is your son!
    LANDGRAVE. Oh that he ne'er were born!
Hola! Halberdiers! Yeomen of the Guard!
(*Enter Guardsmen.*) Bear off this prisoner! Let him sigh out
His blasphemous folly in the castle tower,
Until his hair be snow, his fingers claws.
           They seize and bear away Prince William,
Well, what's your counsel?
    SCHNETZEN. Briefly this, my lord.
The Jews of Nordhausen have brewed the Prince

A love-elixir—let them perish all!

(Tumult without. Singing of Hymns and Ringing of Church-bells. The Landgrave and Schnetzen go to the window.)

*Song (without.)

The cruel pestilence arrives,
Cuts off a myriad human lives.
See the flagellants' naked skin !
They scourge themselves for grievous sin.
Trembles the earth beneath God's breath,
The Jews shall all be burned to death.

LANDGRAVE. Look, foreign pilgrims! What an endless file!
Naked waist-upward. Blood is trickling down
Their lacerated flesh. What do they carry?
SCHNETZEN. Their scourges—iron-pointed, leathern thongs.
Mark how they lash themselves—the strict Flagellants.
The Brothers of the Cross—hark to their cries!
VOICE FROM BELOW. Atone, ye mighty! God is wroth! Expel
The enemies of heaven—raze their homes!

(Confused cries from below which gradually die away in the distance)

Woe to God's enemies! Death to the Jews!
They poison all our wells—they bring the plague.
Kill them who killed our Lord! Their homes shall be
A wilderness—drown them in their own blood!

(The Landgrave and Schnetzen withdraw from the window.)

SCHNETZEN. Do not the people ask the same as I?
Is not the people's voice the voice of God?
LANDGRAVE.   I will consider.
SCHNETZEN.   Not too long, my liege.
The moment favors. Later 'twere hard to show
Due cause to his Imperial Majesty,
For slaughtering the vassals of the Crown.
Two mighty friends are theirs. His holiness
Clement the Sixth and Kaiser Karl.
LANDGRAVE.   'Twere rash
Contending with such odds.
SCHNETZEN.   Courage, my lord.
These battle singly against death and fate.
Your allies are the sense and heart o' the world.
Priests war-ing for their Christ, nobles for gold,
And peoples for the very breath of life
Spoiled by the poison-mixers. Kaiser Karl
Lifts his lone voice unheard, athwart the roar
Of such a flood; the papal bull is whirled
An unconsidered rag amidst the eddies.
LANDGRAVE. What credence lend you to the general rumor

---

* A Rhyme of the Times. See Graetz' History of the Jews, Page 374, Vol. 7.

Of the river poison?

SCHNETZEN. Such as mine eyes avouch.
I have seen, yea touched the leathern wallet found
On the body of one from whom the truth was wrenched
By salutary torture. He confessed,
Though but a famulus of the master-wizard,
The horrible old Moses of Mayence,
He had flung such pouches in the Rhine. the Elbe,
The Oder, Danube—in a hundred brooks,
Until the wholesome air reeked pestilence;
'Twas an ell long, filled with a dry, fine dust
Of rusty black and red, deftly compounded
Of powdered flesh of basilisks, spiders, frogs,
And lizards, baked with sacramental dough
In Christian blood.

LANDGRAVE. Such goblin-tales may curdle
The veins of priest-rid women, fools and children.
They are not for the ears of sober men.

SCHNETZEN. Pardon me, Sire. I am a simple soldier.
My God, my conscience, and my suzerain,
These are my guides—blindfold I follow them.
If your keen royal wit pierce the gross web
Of common superstition—be not wroth
At your poor vassal's loyal ignorance.
Remember, too, Süsskind retains your bonds.
The old fox will not press you; he would bleed
Against the native instinct of the Jew,
Rather his last gold doit, and so possess
Your ease of mind. nag, chafe and toy with it;
Abide his natural death, and other Jews
Less devilish-cunning. franklier Hebrew-viced,
Will claim redemption of your pledge.

LANDGRAVE. How know you
That Süsskind holds my bonds?

SCHNETZEN. You think the Jews
Keep such things secret? Not a Jew but knows
Your debt exact—the sum and date of interest
And that you visit Susskind, not for love,
But for his shekels.

LANDGRAVE. Well. the Jews shall die.
This is the will of God. Whom shall I send
To bear my message to the council?

SCHNETZEN. I
Am ever at your 'hest. To-morrow morn
Sees me in Nordhausen.

LANDGRAVE. Come two hours hence.
I will deliver you the letter signed.
Make ready for your ride.

SCHNETZEN. (*kisses Frederick's hand.*) Farewell, my master.
(*aside.*) Ah vengeance cometh late, Süsskind von Orb,
But yet it comes! My wife was burned through thee,
Thou and thy children are consumed by me!

Exit.

SCENE II. A Room in the Wartburg Monastery. Princess Mathildis and Prior
Peppercorn.

PRIOR. Be comforted, my daughter. Your lord's wisdom
Goes hand in hand with his known piety
Thus dealing with your son. To love a Jewess
Is flat contempt of heaven— to ask in marriage,
Sheer spiritual suicide. Let be;
Justice must take its course.
PRINCESS.   Justice is murdered;
Oh slander not her corpse. For my son's fault,
A thousand innocents are doomed. Is that
God's justice?
PRIOR.   Yea, our liege is but His servant.
Did not He purge with fiery hail those twain
Blotches of festering sin, Gomorrah, Sodom?
The Jews are never innocent,—when Christ
Agonized on the Cross, they cried—" His blood
Be on our children's heads and ours!" I mark
A dangerous growing evil of these days,
Pity, misnamed—say, criminal indulgence
Of reprobates brow-branded by the Lord.
Shall we excel the Christ in charity?
Because His law is love, we tutor him
In mercy and reward his murderers?
Justice is blind and virtue is austere.
If the true passion brimmed our yearning hearts
The vision of the agony would loom
Fixed vividly between the day and us;—
Nailed on the gaunt black Cross the divine form,
Wax-white and dripping blood from ankles, wrists,
The sacred ichor that redeems the world,
And crowded in strange shadow of eclipse.
Reviling Jews. wagging their heads accursed,
Sputtering blasphemy—who then would shrink
From holy vengeance? who would offer less
Heroic wrath and filial zeal to God
Than to a murdered father?
PRINCESS.   But my son
Will die with her he loves.
PRIOR.   Better to perish
In time than in eternity. No question
Pends here of individual life; our sight

Must broaden to embrace the scope sublime
Of this trans-earthly theme.   The Jew survives
Sword, plague, fire, cataclysm—and must, since Christ
Cursed him to live till doomsday, still to be
A scarecrow to the nations.   None the less
Are we beholden in Christ's name at whiles,
When maggot-wise Jews breed, infest, infect
Communities of Christians, to wash clean
The Church's vesture, shaking off the filth
That gathers round her skirts.   A perilous germ!
Know you not, all the wells, the very air
The Jews have poisoned?—Through their arts alone
The Black Death scourges Christendom.
    PRINCESS.   I know
All heinousness imputed by their foes.
Father, mistake me not: I urge no plea
To shield this hell-spawn, loathed by all who love
The lamb and kiss the Cross.   I had not guessed
Such obscure creatures crawled upon my path,
Had not my son—I know not how misled
Deigned to ennoble with his great regard,
A sparkle midst the dust motes.   *She* is sacred.
What is her tribe to me?   Her kith and kin
May rot or roast—the Jews of Nordhausen
May hang, drown. perish like the Jews of France,
But she shall live—Liebhaid von Orb, the Jewess,
The Prince, my son, elects to love.
    PRIOR.   Amen!
Washed in baptismal waters she shall be
Led like the clean-fleeced yeanling to the fold.
Trust me, my daughter—for through me the Church
Which is the truth, which is the life, doth speak.
Yet first 'twere best essay to cure the Prince
Of his moon-fostered madness, bred, no doubt,
By baneful potions which these cunning knaves
Are skilled to mix.
    PRINCESS.   Go visit him, dear father,
Where in the high tower mewed, a wing-clipped eagle,
His spirit breaks in cage.   You are his master,
He is wont from childhood to hear wisdom fall
From your instructed lips.   Tell him his mother
Rises not from her knees, till he is freed.
    PRIOR.   Madam, I go.   Our holy Church has healed
Far deadlier heart-wounds than a love-sick boy's.
Be of good cheer, the Prince shall live to bless
The father's rigor who kept pure of blot
A 'scutcheon more unsullied than the sun.
    PRINCESS.   Thanks and farewell.

PRIOR. Farewell. God send thee peace!
(Exeunt.)

SCENE III. A mean apartment in one of the Towers of the Landgrave's Palace.
PRINCE WILLIAM discovered seated at the window.

PRINCE W. The slow sun sets; with lingering, large embrace
He folds the enchanted hill; then like a god
Strides into heaven behind the purple peak.
Oh beautiful! In the clear, rayless air,
I see the chequered vale mapped far below,
The sky-paved streams, the velvet pasture slopes,
The grim, gray cloister whose deep vesper bell
Blends at this height with tinkling, homebound herds!
I see—but oh, how far!—the blessed town
Where Liebhaid dwells. Oh that I were yon star
That pricks the West's unbroken foil of gold,
Bright as an eye, only to gaze on her!
How keen it sparkles o'er the Venusburg!
When brown night falls and mists begin to live,
Then will the phantom hunting-train emerge.
Hounds straining, black fire-eyeballed, breathless steeds,
Spurred by wild huntsmen, and unhallowed nymphs,
And at their head the foam-begotten witch,
Of soul-destroying beauty. Saints of heaven!
Preserve mine eyes from such unholy sight!
How all unlike the base desire which leads
Misguided men to that infernal cave,
Is the pure passion that exalts my soul
Like a religion! Yet Christ pardon me,
If this be sin to thee!

(He takes his lute, and begins to sing. Enter with a lamp Steward of the Castle,
followed by Prior Peppercorn. Steward lays down the lamp and exit.)

Good even, father!
PRIOR. Benedicite!
Our bird makes merry his dull bars with song,
Yet would not penitential psalms accord
More fitly with your sin than minstrels' lays?
PRINCE W. I know no blot upon my life's fair record.
PRIOR. What is it to wanton with a Christ-cursed Jewess,
Defy thy father and pollute thy name,
And fling to the ordures thine immortal soul?
PRINCE W. Forbear! thy cowl's a helmet, thy serge frock
Invulnerable as brass—yet I am human,
Thou, priest, art still a man.
PRIOR. Pity him, heaven!
To what a pass their draughts have brought the mildest,
Noblest of princes! Softly, my son; be ruled
By me, thy spiritual friend and father.

Thou hast been drugged with sense-deranging potions,
Thy blood set boiling and thy brain askew;
When these thick fumes subside, thou shalt awake
To bless the friend who gave thy madness bounds.
    PRINCE W. Madness! Yea, as the sane world goes, I am mad.
What else to help the helpless, to uplift
The low, to adore the good, the beautiful,
To live, battle, suffer, die for truth, for love!
But that is wide of the question. Let me hear
What you are charged to impart—my father's will.
    PRIOR. Heart-cleft by his dear offspring's shame, he prays
Your reason be restored, your wayward sense
Renew its due allegiance. For his son
He, the good parent weeps—hot drops of gall,
Wrung from a spirit seldom eased by tears.
But for his honor pricked, the Landgrave takes
Most just and general vengeance.
    PRINCE W.   In the name of God,
What has he done to *her?*
    PRIOR.   Naught, naught,—as yet.
Sweet Prince, be calm; you leap like flax to flame.
You nest within your heart a cockatrice,
Pluck it from out your bosom and breathe pure
Of the filthy egg. The Landgrave brooks no more
The abomination that infects his town.
The Jews of Nordhausen are doomed.
    PRINCE W.   Alack!
Who and how many of that harmless tribe,
Those meek and pious men have been elected
To glut with innocent blood the oppressor's wrath?
    PRIOR. Who should go free where equal guilt is shared?
Frederick is just—they perish all at once,
Generous moreover—for in their mode of death
He grants them choice.
    PRINCE W.   My father had not lost
The human semblance when I saw him last.
Nor can he be divorced in this short space
From his shrewd wit. How shall he make provision
For the vast widowed, orphaned host this deed
Burdens the state withal?
    PRIOR.   Oh excellent!
This is the crown of folly, topping all!
Forgive me, Prince, when I gain breath to point
Your comic blunder, you will laugh with me.
Patience—I'll draw my chin as long as yours.
Well, 'twas my fault—one should be accurate—
Jews, said I? when I meant Jews, Jewesses,
And Jewlings! all betwixt the age

Of twenty-four hours, and of five score years.
Of either sex, of every known degree,
All the contaminating vermin purged
With one clean, searching blast of wholesome fire.
    PRINCE W, Oh Christ, disgraced, insulted! Horrible man,
Remembered be your laugh in lowest hell,
Dragging you to the nether pit! Forgive me;
You are my friend—take me from here —unbolt
Those iron doors—I'll crawl upon my knees
Unto my father—I have much to tell him.
For but the freedom of one hour, sweet Prior,
I'll brim the vessels of the Church with gold.
    PRIOR. Boy! your bribes touch not, nor your curses shake
The minister of Christ. Yet I will bear
Your message to the Landgrave.
    PRINCE W.   Whet your tongue
Keen as the archangel's blade of truth— your voice
Be as God's thunder, and your heart one blaze—
Then can you speak my cause. With me, it needs
No plausive gift; the smitten head, stopped throat
Blind eyes and silent suppliance of sorrow
Persuade beyond all eloquence. Great God!
Here while I rage and beat against my bars,
The infernal fagots may be stacked for her,
The hell-spark kindled. Go to him, dear Prior,
Speak to him gently, be not too much moved,
'Neath its rude case you had ever a soft heart,
And he is stirred by mildness more than passion.
Recall to him her round, clear, ardent eyes,
The shower of sunshine that's her hair, the sheen
Of the cream-white flesh—shall these things serve as fuel?
Tell him that when she heard once he was wounded,
And how he bled and anguished; at the tale
She wept for pity.
    PRIOR.   If her love be true
She will adore her lover's God, embrace
The faith that marries you in life and death.
This promise with the Landgrave would prevail
More than all sobs and pleadings.
    PRINCE W.   Save her, save her!
If any promise, vow or oath can serve,
Oh trusting, tranquil Süsskind, who estopped
Your ears forewarned, bandaged your visioned eyes,
To woo destruction! Stay! did he not speak
Of amulet or talisman? These horrors
Have crowded out my wits. Yea, the gold casket!
What fixed serenity beamed from his brow,
Laying the precious box within my hands!

[He brings from the shelf the casket, and hands it to the Prior.]

Deliver this unto the Prince my father,
Nor lose one vital moment. What it holds,
I guess not—but my light heart whispers me
The jewel safety's locked beneath its lid.
  PRIOR.   First I must foil such devil's tricks as lurk
In its gem-crusted cabinet.
  PRINCE   Away!
Deliverance posts on your return   I feel it.
For your much comfort thanks.   Goodnight.
  PRIOR.   Goodnight.

Exit.

END OF SECOND ACT.

ACT III.

A cell in the Wartburg Monastery.   Enter Prior Peppercorn with the casket.

  PRIOR.   So! Glittering shell where doubtless shines concealed
An orient treasure fit to bribe a king,
Ransom a prince and buy him for a son.
I have baptized thee now before the altar,
Effaced the Jew's contaminating touch,
And I am free to claim the Church's tithe
From thy receptacle. (*He is about to unlock the casket, when, enters
Lay Brother, and he hastily conceals it.*)
  LAY BROTHER.   Peace be thine, father!
  PRIOR.   Amen! and thine.   What's new?
  LAY BROTHER.   A strange Flagellant
Fresh come to Wartburg craves a word with thee.
  PRIOR.   Bid him within. (*Exit Lay Brother. Prior places the cas
ket in a Cabinet*) Patience! No hour of the day
Brings freedom to the priest.

(Re-enter Lay Brother ushering in Nordmann—and exit.)

                          Brother, all hail!
Blessed be thou who comest in God's name!
  NORDMANN.   May the Lord grant thee thine own prayer four-fold!
  PRIOR.   What is thine errand?
  NORDMANN.   Look at me, my father.
Long since you called me friend.

(The Prior looks at him attentively, while an expression of wonder and terror gradually overspreads his face.)
  PRIOR.   Almighty God!
The grave gives up her dead.   Thou canst not be—
  NORDMANN.   Nordmann of Nordmannstein,the Knight of Treffurt.
  PRIOR.   He was beheaded years agone.

NORDMANN. His death
Had been decreed, but in his stead a squire
Clad in his garb and masked, paid bloody forfeit.
A loyal wretch on whom the Prince wreaked vengeance,
Rather than publish the true bird had flown.
   PRIOR. Does Frederick know thou art in Eisenach?
   NORDMANN. Who would divine the Knight of Nordmannstein
In the Flagellants' weeds? From land to land,
From town to town, we cry, "Death to the Jews!
Hep! hep! *Hierosolyma Est Perdita!*"
They die like rats; in Gotha they are burned;
Two of the devil brutes in Chatelard,
Child-murderefs, wizards, breeders of the Plague,
Had the truth squeezed from them with screws and racks,
All with explicit date, place, circumstance,
And written as it fell from dying lips
By scriveners of the law. On their confession
The Jews of Savoy were destroyed. To-morrow noon
The holy flames shall dance in Nordhausen.
   PRIOR. Your zeal bespeaks you fair. In your deep eyes,
A mystic fervor shines; yet your scarred flesh
And shrunken limbs denote exhausted nature,
Collapsing under discipline.
   NORDMANN. Speak not
Of the degrading body and its pangs.
I am all zeal, all energy, all spirit.
Jesus was wroth at me, at all the world,
For our indulgence of the flesh, our base
Compounding with his enemies the Jews.
But at Madonna Mary's intercession,
He charged an angel with this gracious word,
"Whoso will scourge himself for forty days,
And labor towards the clean extermination
Of earth s corrupting vermin, shall be saved."
Oh, what vast peace this message brought my soul!
I have learned to love the ecstasy of pain.
When the sweat stands upon my flesh, the blood
Throbs in my bursting veins, my twisted muscles
Are cramped with agony, I seem to crawl
Anigh his feet who suffered on the Cross.
   PRIOR. Oh all transforming Time! Can this be he,
The iron warrior of a decade since,
The gallant youth of earlier years, whose pranks
And reckless buoyancy of temper flashed
Clear sunshine through my gloom?
   NORDMANN. I am unchanged,
(Save that the spirit of grace has fallen on me.)
Urged by one motive through these banished years,

Fed by one hope, awake to realize
One living dream—my long delayed revenge.
You saw the day when Henry Schnetzen's castle
Was razed with fire?
    PRIOR.   I saw it.
    NORDMANN.   Schnetzen's wife,
Three days a mother, perished.
    PRIOR.   And his child?
    NORDMANN. His child was saved.
    PRIOR.   By whom?
    NORDMANN.   By the same Jew
Who had betrayed the Castle.
    PRIOR.   Süsskind von Orb?
    NORDMANN.   Süsskind von Orb! and Schnetzen's daughter lives
As the Jew's child within the Judengasse.
    PRIOR.   (*eagerly*) What proof hast thou of this?
    NORDMANN.   Proof of these eyes!
I visited von Orb to ask a loan.
There saw I such a maiden as no Jew
Was ever blessed withal since Jesus died.
White as a dove, with hair like golden floss,
Eyes like an Alpine lake. The haughty line
Of brow imperial, high bridged nose, fine chin,
Seemed like the shadow cast upon the wall,
Where Lady Schnetzen stood.
    PRIOR.   Why hast thou ne'er
Discovered her to Schnetzen?
    NORDMANN.   He was my friend.
I shared with him thirst, hunger, sword and fire.
But he became a courtier. When the Margrave
Sent me his second challenge to the field,
His messenger was Schnetzen! 'Mongst his knights,
The apple of his eye was Henry Schnetzen.
He was the hound that hunted me to death.
He stood by Frederick's side when I was led
Bound, to the presence. I denounced him coward,
He smote me on the cheek. Christ! it stings yet.
He hissed—" My liege, let Henry Nordmann hang!
He is no knight, for he receives a blow,
Nor dare avenge it!" My gyved wrists moved not,
No nerve twitched in my face, although I felt
Flame leap there from my heart, then flying back,
Leave it cold-bathed with deathly ooze—my soul
In silence took her supreme vow of hate.
    PRIOR.   Praise be to God that thou hast come to-day.
To-morrow were too late. Hast thou not heard
Frederick sends Schnetzen unto Nordhausen,
With fire and torture for the Jews?

NORDMANN.   So! Henry Schnetzen
Shall be the Jews' destroyer?   Ah!

PRIOR.   One moment.
Mayhap this box which Susskind sends the Prince
Reveals more wonders.   *He brings forth the Casket from the Cabi-*
net—opens it, and discovers a golden cross and a parchment which he
hastily overlooks.)   Hark! your word's confirmed
Blessed be Christ, our Lord!   (*reads.*)

" I Süsskind von Orb of Nordhausen, swear by the unutterable Name, that on the
day when the Castle of Salza was burned, I rescued the infant daughter of Henry
Schnetzen from the flames.   I purposed restoring her to her father, but when I re-
turned to Nordhausen, I found my own child lying on her bier, and my wife in fe-
vered frenzy calling for her babe.   I sought the leech, who counseled me to show
the Christian child to the bereaved mother as her own.   The pious trick prevailed;
the fever broke, the mother was restored.   But never would she part with the child,
even when she had learned to whom it belonged, and until she was gathered with the
dead—may peace be with her soul!—she fostered in our Jewish home the offspring of
the Gentile knight.   Then again would I have yielded the girl to her parent, but
Schnetzen was my foe, and I feared the haughty baron would disown the daughter
who came from the hands of the Jew.   Now however the maiden's temporal happiness
demands that she be acknowledged by her rightful father.   Let him see what I have
written.   As a token, behold this golden cross, bound by the Lady Schnetzen round
the infant's neck.   May the God of Abraham, Isaac and Jacob redeem and bless me
as I have writ the truth."

PRIOR.   I thank the Saints that this has come betimes.
Thou shalt renounce thy hate.   Vengeance is mine,
The Lord hath said.

NORDMANN.   Oh! all transforming Time!
Is this meek, saintly-hypocrite, the firm
Ambitious, resolute Reinhard Peppercorn,
Terror of Jews and beacon of the Church?
Look, you, I have won the special grace of Christ,
He knows through what fierce anguish!   Now he leans
Out of his heaven to whisper in mine ear,
And reach me my revenge.   He makes my cause
His own—and I shall fail upon these heights,
Sink from the level of a hate sublime,
To puerile pity!

PRIOR.   Be advised.   You hold
Your enemy's living heart within your hands.
This secret is far costlier than you dreamed,
For Frederick's son woos Schnetzen's daughter.   See,
A hundred delicate springs your wit may move,
Your puppets are the Landgrave and the Prince,
The Governor of Salza and the Jews.
You may recover station, wealth and honor,
Selling your secret shrewdly; while rash greed
Of clumsy vengeance may but drag you down
In the wild whirl of universal ruin.

NORDMANN.   Christ teach me whom to trust!   I would not spill

One drop from out this brimming glorious cup
For which my parched heart pants.   I will consider.
   PRIOR.   Pardon me now, if I break off our talk.
Let all rest as it stands until the dawn.
I have many orisons before the light.
   NORDMANN.   Goodnight, true friend.   Devote a prayer to me.
(*Aside.*) I will outwit you, serpent, though you glide
Athwart the dark, noiseless and swift as fate.
Exit.

SCENE II.   On the road to Nordhausen.   Moonlit, rocky landscape.   On the right
between high, white cliffs a narrow stream spanned by a wooden bridge.   Thick
bushes and trees.   Enter PRINCE WILLIAM and PAGE.
   PRINCE W.   Is this the place where we shall find fresh steeds?
Would I had not dismounted!
   PAGE.   Nay, sir; beyond
The Werra bridge the horses wait for us.
These rotten planks would never bear their weight.
   PRINCE W.   When I am Landgrave these things shall be cared for.
This is an ugly spot for travelers
To loiter in.   How swift the water runs,
Brawling above our voices.   Human cries
Would never reach Liborius' convent yonder,
Perched on the sheer, chalk cliff.   I think of peril,
From my excess of joy   My spirit chafes,
She that would breast broad-winged the air, must halt
On stumbling mortal limbs.   Look, thither, boy,
How the black shadows of the tree-boles stripe
The moon-blanched bridge and meadow.
   PAGE.   Sir, what's that?
Yon stir and glitter in the bush?
   PRINCE W.   The moon
Pricking the dewdrops, plays fantastic tricks
With objects most familiar.   Look again,
And where thou sawst the steel-blue flicker glint,
Thou findst a black, wet leaf.
   PAGE.   No, no! oh God!
Your sword, sir!   Treason!
   (Four armed masked men leap from out the bush, seize, bind and overmaster, after
a brief but violent resistance. the Prince and his servant.)
   PRINCE W.   Who are ye, villains?   lying
In murderous ambush for the Prince of Meissen?
If you be knights, speak honorably your names,
And I will combat you in knightly wise.
If ye be robbers, name forthwith your ransom.
Let me but speed upon my journey now.
By Christ's blood. I beseech you, let me go!
Ho! treason! murder! help!
   (He is dragged off struggling   Exeunt omnes.)

SCENE III. Nordhausen. A room in Süsskind's house. Liebhaid and Claire.

LIEBHAID. Say on, poor girl, if but to speak these horrors
Revive not too intense a pang.
  CLAIRE.   Not so.
For all my woes seem here to merge their flood
Into a sea of infinite repose.
Through France our journey led, as I have told,
From desolation unto desolation.
Naught stayed my father's course—sword, storm, flame, plague,
Exhaustion of the eighty year old frame.
O'ertaxed beyond endurance. Once, once only,
His divine face succumbed. 'Twas at day's close,
And all the air was one discouragement
Of April snow-flakes. I was drenched, cold, sick,
With weariness and hunger light of head,
And on the open road, suddenly turned
The whole world like the spinning flakes of snow.
My numb hand slipped from his, and all was blank.
His beard, his breath upon my brow. his tears
Scalding my cheek hugged close against his breast,
And in my ear deep groans awoke me. " God!"
I heard him cry—" try me not past my strength.
No prophet I, a blind, old dying man!"
Gently I drew his face to mine, and kissed,
Whispering courage—then his spirit broke
Utterly; shattered were his wits, I feared.
But past is past; he is at peace, and I
Find shelter from the tempest. Tell me rather
Of your serene life.
  LIEBHAID.   Happiness is mute.
What record speaks of placid, golden days,
Matched each with each as twins? Till yester-eve
My life was simple as a song. At whiles
Dark tales have reached us of our people's wrongs,
Strange, far-off anguish, furrowing with fresh care
My father's brow, draping our home with gloom.
We're still blessed; the Landgrave is his friend—
The Prince—my Prince—dear Claire, ask me no more!
My adored enemy, my angel-fiend,
Splitting my heart against my heart! Oh God,
How shall I pray for strength to love him less
Than mine own soul?
  CLAIRE.   What mean these contrary words?
These passionate tears?
  LIEBHAID.   Brave girl, who art inured
To difficult privation and rude pain,
What good shall come forswearing kith and God,

To follow the allurements of the heart?
  CLAIRE. Duty wears one face, but a thousand masks.
Thy feet she leads to glittering peaks, while mine
She guides midst brambled roadways. Not the first
Art thou of Israel's women, chosen of God,
To rule o'er rulers. I remember me
A verse my father often would repeat
Out of our sacred Talmud: '' Every time
The sun, moon, stars begin again their course,
They hesitate, trembling and filled with shame,
Blush at the blasphemous worship offered them,
And each time God's voice thunders, crying out,
On with your duty!''
         (Enter Reuben.)
  REUBEN. Sister, we are lost!
The streets are thronged with panic-stricken folk.
Wild rumors fill the air. Two of our tribe,
Young Mordecai, as I hear, and old Baruch,
Seized by the mob, were dragged towards Eisenach,
Cruelly used, left to bleed out their lives,
In the wayside ditch at night. This morn, betimes,
The iron-hearted Governor of Salza,
Rides furious into Nordhausen; his horse
Spurred past endurance, drops before the gate.
The Council has been called to hear him read
The Landgrave's message,— all men say, 'tis death
Unto our race.
  LIEBHAID. Where is our father, Reuben?
  REUBEN. With Rabbi Jacob. Through the streets they walk,
Striving to quell the terror Ah, too late!
Had he but heeded the prophetic voice,
This warning angel led to us in vain!
  LIEBHAID. Brother, be calm. Man your young heart to front
Whatever ills the Lord afflicts us with.
What does Prince William? Hastes he not to aid?
  REUBEN. None know his whereabouts. Some say he's held
Imprisoned by the Landgrave. Others tell
While he was posting with deliverance
To Nordhausen, in bloody Schnetzen's wake,
He was set upon by ruffians—kidnapped—killed.
What do I know—hid till our ruin's wrought,
        (Liebhaid swoons.)
  CLAIRE. Hush, foolish boy. See how your rude words hurt.
Look up, sweet girl; take comfort.
  REUBEN. Pluck up heart;
Dear sister, pardon me; he lives, he lives!
  LIEBHAID. God help me! Shall my heart crack for love's loss
That meekly bears my people's martyrdom?

He lives—I feel it—to live or die with me.
I love him as my soul—no more of that.
I am all Israel's now—till this cloud pass,
I have no thought, no passion, no desire,
Save for my people

(Enter Süsskind.)

SUSSKIND.   Blessed art thou, my child!
This is the darkest hour before the dawn.
Thou art the morning star of Israel.
How dear thou art to me—heart of my heart,
Mine, mine, all mine to-day! the pious thought,
The orient spirit mine, the Jewish soul.
The glowing veins that sucked life-nourishment
From Hebrew mother's milk.   Look at me, Liebhaid,
Tell me you love me   Pity me, my God!
No fiercer pang than this did Jephthah know.
    LIEBHAID.   Father, what wild and wandering words are these?
Is all hope lost?
    SUSSKIND.   Nay, God is good to us.
I am so well assured the town is safe,
That I can weep my private loss—of thee.
An ugly dream I had, quits not my sense,
That you, made Princess of Thuringia,
Forsook your father, and forswore your race.
Forgive me, Liebhaid, I am calm again,
We must be brave—I who besought my tribe
To bide their fate in Nordhausen, and you
Whom God elects for a peculiar lot.
With many have I talked; some crouched at home,
Some wringing hands about the public ways.
I gave all comfort   I am very weary.
My children, we had best go in and pray,
Solace and safety dwell but in the Lord.

(Exeunt.)

END OF THIRD ACT.

ACT IV.

SCENE I. The City Hall at Nordhausen. Deputies and Burghers assembling. To the right at a table near the President's chair, is seated the Public Scrivener. Enter DIETRICH VON TETTENBORN, and HENRY SCHNETZEN with an open letter in his hand.

SCHNETZEN. Didst hear the fellow's words who handed it?
I asked from whom it came, he spoke by rote,
" The pepper bites, the corn is ripe for harvest,
I come from Eisenach." 'Tis some tedious jest.

TETTENBORN. Doubtless your shrewd friend Prior Peppercorn
Masks here some warning. Ask the scrivener
To help us to its contents.

SCHNETZEN. (*To the clerk.*) Read me these.

SCRIVENER (*reads*):
" Beware, Lord Henry Schnetzen, of Süsskind's lying tongue! He will thrust a cuckoo's egg into your nest.
[Signed]   ONE WHO KNOWS."

SCHNETZEN. A cuckoo's egg! that riddle puzzles me;
But this I know. Schnetzen is no man's dupe,
Much less a Jew's.

(Schnetzen and von Tettenborn take their seats side by side.)

TETTENBORN. Knights, counsellors and burghers!
Sir Henry Schnetzen, Governor of Salza,
Comes on grave mission from His Highness Frederick,
Margrave of Meissen, Landgrave of Thuringia,
Our town's imperial Patron and Protector.

SCHNETZEN. Gentles, I greet you in the Landgrave's name,
The honored bearer of his princely script,
Sealed with his signet. Read, good Master Clerk.

[He hands a parchment to the Scrivener, who reads aloud:]
Lord President and Deputies of the town of Nordhausen! Know that we, Frederick, Margrave of Meissen, and Landgrave of Thuringia, command to be burned all the Jews within our territories as far as our lands extend, on account of the great crime they have committed against Christendom in throwing poison into the wells, of the truth of which indictment we have absolute knowledge. Therefore we admonish you to have the Jews killed in honor of God, so that Christendom be not enfeebled by them. Whatever responsibility you incur, we will assume with our Lord the Emperor, and with all other lords. Know also that we send to you Henry Schnetzen, our Governor of Salza, who shall publicly accuse your Jews of the above-mentioned crime. Therefore we beseech you to help him to do justice upon them, and we will singularly reward your good will.
Given at Eisenach, the Thursday after St. Walpurgis, under our secret seal.†

A COUNSELLOR (*Diether von Werther.*) Fit silence welcomes this unheard-of wrong !
So! Ye are men—free, upright, honest men,
Not hired assassins? I half doubted it,

† This is an authentic document.

Seeing you lend these infamous words your ears.

SCHNETZEN.   Consider, gentlemen of Nordhausen,
Ere ye give heed to the rash partisan.
Ye cros̱s the Landgrave—well? he crosses you.
It may be I shall ride to Nordhausen,
Not with a harmless script, but with a sword,
And so denounce the town for perjured vow.
What was the Strasburg citizens' reward
Who championed these lost wretches, in the face
Of King and Kaiser—three against the world,
Conrad von Winterthur the Burgomaster,
Deputy Gosse Sturm, and Peter Schwarber,
Master mechanic?   These leagued fools essayed
To stand between the people's sacred wrath,
And its doomed object.   Well, the Jews. no less,
Were rooted from the city neck and crop,
And their three friends degraded from their rank
I' the city council, glad to save their skins.
The Jews are foes to God.   Our Holy Father
Thunders his ban from Rome against all such
As aid the poisoners.   Your oath to God,
And to the Prince enjoins—Death to the Jews.

A BURGHER.   (*Reinhard Rolapp.*)   Why all this vain debate? The
    Landgrave's brief
Affirms the Jews fling poison in the wells.
Shall we stand by and leave them unmolested,
Till they have made our town a wilderness?
I say, Death to the Jews!

A BURGHER.   (*Hugo Schultz.*)My lord and brethren,
I have scant gift of speech, ye are all my elders.
Yet hear me for truth's sake, and liberty's.
The Landgrave of Thuringia is our patron,
True—and our town's imperial Governor,
But are we not free burghers?   Shall we not
Debate and act in freedom?   If Lord Schnetzen
Will force our council with the sword—enough!
We are not frightened schoolboys crouched beneath
The master's rod, but men who bear the sword
As brave as he.   By this grim messenger,
Send back this devilish missive.   Say to Frederick
Nordhausen never was enfeoffed to him.
Prithee, Lord President, bid Henry Schnetzen
Withdraw awhile, that we may all take counsel,
According to the hour's necessity.
As free men, whom nor fear nor favor swerves.

TETTENBORN.   Bold youth, you err.   True, Nordhausen is free,
And God be witness, we for fear or favor,

Would never shed the blood of innocence.
But here the Prince condemns the Jews to death
For capital crime.   Who sees a snake must kill,
Ere it spit fatal venom.   I, too, say
Death to the Jews!
    ALL.   Death to the Jews!   God wills it!
    TETTENBORN.   Give me your voices in the urn.
(*The votes are taken.*)   One voice
For mercy, all the rest for death. (*To an usher.*)   Go thou
To the Jews' quarter; bid Süsskind von Orb,
And Rabbi Jacob hither to the Senate,
To hear the Landgrave's and the town's decree. (*Exit Usher.*)
(*To Schnetzen.*) What learn you of this evil through the State?
    SCHNETZEN.   It swells to monstrous bulk.   In many towns,
Folk build high ramparts, round the wells and springs.
In some they shun the treacherous sparkling brooks,
To drink dull rain-water, or melted snow,
In mountain districts.   Frederick has been patient,
And too long clement, duped by fleece-cloaked wolves.
But now his subjects' clamor rouses him
To front the general peril.   As I hear,
A fiendish and far-reaching plot involves
All Christian thrones and peoples.   These vile vermin,
Burrowing underneath society,
Have leagued with Moors in Spain, with heretics
Too plentiful—Christ knows! in every land,
And planned a subterraneous, sinuous scheme,
To overthrow all Christendom.   But see,
Where with audacious brows, and steadfast mien,
They enter, bold as innocence.   Now listen,
For we shall hear brave falsehoods.
               (Enter Süsskind von Orb and Rabbi Jacob.)
    TETTENBORN.   Rabbi Jacob,
And thou, Süsskind von Orb, bow down, and learn
The Council's pleasure.   You the least despised
By true believers, and most reverenced
By your own tribe, we grace with our free leave
To enter, yea, to lift your voices here,
Amid these wise and honorable men,
If ye find aught to plead, that mitigates
The just severity of your doom.   Our Prince,
Frederick the Grave, Patron of Nordhausen,
Ordains that all the Jews within his lands,
For the foul crime of poisoning the wells,
Bringing the Black Death upon Christendom,
Shall be consumed with flame.
    RABBI JACOB.   (*Springing forward and clasping his hands*), I' the
    Name of God,

Your God and ours, have mercy!
   SUSSKIND.   Noble lords,
Burghers and artisans of Nordhausen,
Wise, honorable, just, God-fearing men,
Shall ye condemn or ever ye have heard?
Sure, one at least owns here the close, kind name
Of Brother—unto him I turn. At least
Some sit among you who have wedded wives,
Bear the dear title and the precious charge
Of husband—unto these I speak. Some here,
Are crowned, it may be, with the sacred name
Of Father—unto these I pray. All, all
Are sons—all have been children, all have known
The love of parents—unto these I cry:
Have mercy on us, we are innocent,
Who are brothers, husbands, fathers, sons as ye!
Look you, we have dwelt among you many years,
Led thrifty, peaceable, well-ordered lives,
Who can attest, who prove we ever wrought
Or ever did devise the smallest harm,
Far less this fiendish crime against the State?
Rather let those arise who owe the Jews
Some debt of unpaid kindness, profuse alms,
The Hebrew leech's serviceable skill,
Who know our patience under injury,
And ye would see, if all stood bravely forth,
A motley host, led by the Landgrave's self,
Recruited from all ranks, and in the rear,
The humblest, veriest wretch in Nordhausen.
We know the Black Death is a scourge of God.
Is not our flesh as capable of pain,
Our blood as quick envenomed as your own?
Has the Destroying Angel passed the posts
Of Jewish doors—to visit Christian homes?
We all are slaves of one tremen ous Hour.
We drink the waters which our enemies say
We spoil with poison,—we must breathe, as ye,
The universal air,—we drop, faint, sicken,
From the same causes to the selfsame end.
Ye are not strangers to me, though ye wear
Grim masks to-day—lords, knights and citizens,
Few do I see whose hand has pressed not mine,
In cordial greeting. Dietrich von Tettenborn,
If at my death, my wealth be confiscate
Unto the State, bethink you, lest she prove
A harsher creditor than I have been.
Stout Meister Rolapp, may you never again
Languish so nigh to death that Simon's art

Be needed to restore your lusty limbs.
Good Hugo Schultz—ah! be those blessed tears
Remembered unto you in Paradise!
Look there, my lords, one of your council weeps,
If you be men, why, then an angel sits
On yonder bench. You have good cause to weep,
You who are Christian, and disgraced in that
Whereof you made your boast. I have no tears.
A fiery wrath has scorched their source, a voice
Shrills through my brain—"Not upon us, on them
Fall everlasting woe, if this thing be!"
    SCHNETZEN. My lords of Nordhausen, shall ye be stunned
With sounding words? Behold the serpent's skin,
Sleek-shining, clear as sunlight; yet his tooth
Holds deadly poison Even as the Jews
Did nail the Lord of heaven on the Cross.
So will they murder all his followers.
When once they have the might. Beware, beware!
    SUSSKIND. So *you* are the accuser, my lord Schnetzen?
Now I confess. before you I am guilty.
You are in all this presence, the one man
Whom any Jew hath wronged—and I that Jew.
Oh, my offence is grievous; punish me
With the utmost rigor of the law, for theft
And violence, whom ye deemed an honest man.
But leave my tribe unharmed! I yield my hands
Unto your chains, my body to your fires;
Let one life serve for all.
    SCHNETZEN. You hear, my lords,
How the prevaricating villain shrinks
From the absolute truth, yet dares not front his Maker
With the full damnable lie hot on his lips.
Not thou alone, my private foe shalt die,
But all thy race. Thee had my vengeance reached,
Without appeal to Prince or citizen.
Silence! my heart is cuirassed as my breast.
    RABBI JACOB. Bear with us, gracious lords! My friend is stunned.
He is an honest man. Even I, as 'twere,
Am stupefied by this surprising news.
Yet, let me think—it seems it is not new,
This is an ancient, well-remembered pain.
What, brother, came not one who prophesied
This should betide exactly as it doth?
That was a shrewd old man! Your pardon, lords,
I think you know not just what you would do.
You say the Jews shall burn—shall burn you say;
Why, good my lords, the Jews are not a flock
Of gallows-birds, they are a colony

Of kindly, virtuous folk. Come home with me;
I'll show you happy hearths, glad roofs, pure lives.
Why, some of them are little quick-eyed boys,
Some, pretty, ungrown maidens—children's children
Of those who called me to the pastorate.
And some are beautiful tall girls, some, youths
Of marvelous promise, some are old and sick,
Amongst them there be mothers, infants, brides,
Just like your Christian people, for all the world.
Know ye what burning is? Hath one of you,
Scorched ever his soft flesh, or singed his beard,
His hair, his eyebrows—felt the keen, fierce nip
Of the pungent flame—and raises not his voice
To stop this holocaust? God! 'tis too horrible!
Wake me, my friends, from this terrific dream.

    SUSSKIND. Courage, my brother. On our firmness hangs
The dignity of Israel. Sir Governor,
I have a secret word to speak with you.

    SCHNETZEN. Ye shall enjoy with me the jest. These knaves
Are apt in quick invention as in crime.
Speak out—I have no secrets from my peers.

    SUSSKIND. My lord, what answer would you give your Christ
If peradventure, in this general doom
You sacrifice a Christian? Some strayed dove
Lost from your cote, among our vultures caged?
Beware, for midst our virgins there is one
Owes kinship nor allegiance to our tribe.
For her dear sake be pitiful, my lords.
Have mercy on our women! Spare at least
My daughter Liebhaid, she is none of mine!
She is a Christian!

    SCHNETZEN. Just as I foretold!
The wretches will forswear the sacred'st ties,
Cringing for life. Serpents, ye all shall die.
So wills the Landgrave; so the court affirms.
Your daughter shall be first, whose wanton arts
Have brought destruction on a princely house.

    SUSSKIND. My lord, be moved. You kill your flesh and blood.
By *Adonai* I swear, your dying wife,
Entrusted to these arms her child. 'Twas I
Carried your infant from your burning home.
Lord Schnetzen, will you murder your own child?

    SCHNETZEN. Ha, excellent! I was awaiting this
Thou wilt inoculate our knightly veins
With thy corrupted Jewish blood. Thou'lt foist
This adder on my bosom. Henry Schnetzen
Is no weak dupe, whom every lie may start.
Make ready, Jew, for death—and warn thy tribe.

SUSSKIND. (*kneeling.*) Is there a God in heaven? I who ne'er
    knelt
Until this hour to any man on earth,
Tyrant, before thee I abase myself.
If one red drop of human blood still flow
In thy congealed veins, if thou e'er have known
Touch of affection, the blind natural instinct
Of common kindred, even beasts partake
Thou man of frozen stone, thou hollow statue,
Grant me one prayer, that thou wilt look on her.
Then shall the eyes of thy dead wife gaze back
From out the maiden's orbs, then shall a voice
Within thine entrails, cry—This is my child.
    SCHNETZEN. Enough! I pray you, my lord President,
End this unseemly scene. This wretched Jew
Would thrust a cuckoo's egg within my nest.
I have had timely warning. Send the twain
Back to their people, that the court's decree
Be published unto all.
    SUSSKIND. Lord Tettenborn!
Citizens! will you see this nameless crime
Brand the clean earth, blacken the crystal heaven?
Why, no man stirs! God! with what thick strange fumes
Hast thou, o' the sudden, brutalized their sense?
Or am I mad? Is this already hell?
Worshipful fiends, I have good store of gold,
Packed in my coffers, or loaned out to—Christians;
I give it you as free as night bestows
Her copious dews—my life shall seal the bond,
Have mercy on my race!
    TETTENBORN. No more, no more!
Go, bid your tribe make ready for their death
At sunset.
    RABBI JACOB. Oh!
    SUSSKIND. At set of sun to-day?
Why, if you traveled to the nighest town,
Summoned to stand before a mortal Prince,
You would need longer grace to put in order
Household effects, to bid farewell to friends,
And make yourself right worthy. But our way
Is long, our journey difficult, our Judge
Of awful majesty. Must we set forth,
Haste-flushed and unprepared? One brief day more,
And all my wealth is yours!
    TETTENBORN. We have heard enough.
Begone, and bear our message.
    SUSSKIND. Courage, brother.
Our fate is sealed. These tigers are athirst.

Return we to our people to proclaim
The gracious sentence of the noble court.
Let us go thank the Lord who made us those
To suffer, not to do, this deed. Be strong.
So! lean on me—we have little time to lose.

(Exeunt.)

END OF ACT FOURTH.

ACT V.

SCENE I. A Room in Süsskind's House. LIEBHAID, CLAIRE, REUBEN.

LIEBHAID. The air hangs sultry as in mid-July.
Look forth, Claire; moves not some big thunder-cloud
Athwart the sky? My heart is sick.
　　CLAIRE. 　　　　　Nay, Liebhaid.
The clear May sun is shining, and the air
Blows fresh and cordial from the budding hills.
　　LIEBHAID. Reuben, what is 't o'clock. Our father stays.
The midday meal was cold an hour agone,
　　REUBEN. 'Tis two full hours past noon: he should be here.
Ah see, he comes. Great God! what woe has chanced?
He totters on his staff; he has grown old
Since he went forth this morn.

Enter SÜSSKIND.)

　　LIEBHAID 　　　Father, what news?
　　SUSSKIND. The Lord have mercy! Vain is the help of man.
Children, is all in order? We must start
At set of sun on a long pilgrimage.
So wills the Landgrave, so the court decrees.
　　LIEBHAID. What is it, father? Exile?
　　SUSSKIND. 　　　　Yea, just that.
We are banished from our vexed, uncertain homes,
'Midst foes and strangers, to a land of peace,
Where joy abides, where only comfort is.
Banished from care, fear, trouble, life—to death
　　REUBEN. Oh horror! horror! Father, I will not die.
Come, let us flee—we yet have time for flight.
I'll bribe the sentinel—he will ope the gates
Liebhaid, Claire, Father! let us flee! Away
To some safe land where we may nurse revenge.
　　SUSSKIND. Courage, my son, and peace. We may not flee.
Didst thou not see the spies who dogged my steps?
The gates are thronged with citizens and guards.
We must not flee—God wills that we should die.

LIEBHAID. Said you at sunset?
SUSSKIND.   So they have decreed.
CLAIRE. Oh why not now? Why spare the time to warn?
Why came they not with thee to massacre,
Leaving no agony betwixt the sentence
And instant execution?   That were mercy!
Oh, my prophetic father!
SUSSKIND.   They allow
Full five hours' grace to shrive our souls with prayer.
We shall assemble in the Synagogue,
As on Atonement Day, confess our sins,
Recite the Kaddish for the Dead, and chant
Our Shibboleth, the Unity of God,
Until the supreme hour when we shall stand
Before the mercy-seat.
LIEBHAID.   In what dread shape
Approaches death?
SUSSKIND.   Nerve your young hearts, my children.
We shall go down as God's three servants went
Into the fiery furnace.   Not again
Shall the flames spare the true-believers' flesh.
The anguish shall be fierce and strong, yet brief.
Our spirits shall not know the touch of pain,
Pure as refined gold they shall issue safe
From the hot crucible; a pleasing sight
Unto the Lord. Oh, 'tis a rosy bed
Where we shall couch, compared with that whereon
They lie who kindle this accursed blaze.
Ye shrink? ye would avert your martyred brows
From the immortal crowns the angels offer?
What! are we Jews and are afraid of death?
God's chosen people, shall we stand a-tremble
Before our Father, as the Gentiles use?
REUBEN.   Shall the smoke choke us, father? or the flame
Consume our flesh?
SUSSKIND.   I know not, boy. Be sure
The Lord will temper the shrewd pain for those
Who trust in Him.
REUBEN.   May I stand by thy side,
And hold my hand in thine until the end?
SUSSKIND.   (aside.)What solace hast thou, God, in all thy heavens
For such an hour as this? Yea, hand in hand
We walk, my son, through fire, to meet the Lord.
Yet there is one among us shall not burn.
A secret shaft long rankling in my heart,
Now I withdraw, and die. Our general doom,
Liebhaid, is not for thee. Thou art no Jewess.

Thy father is the man who wills our death;
Lord Henry Schnetzen.

LIEBHAID.   Look at me! your eyes
Are sane, correcting your distracted words.
This is Love's trick, to rescue me from death.
My love is firm as thine, and dies with thee.

CLAIRE.   Oh, Liebhaid, live.   Hast thou forgot the Prince?
Think of the happy summer blooms for thee
When we are in our graves.

LIEBHAID.   And I shall smile,
Live and rejoice in love, when ye are dead?

SUSSKIND.   My child, my child!   By the Ineffable Name,
The Adonai, I swear, thou must believe,
Albeit thy father scoffed, gave me the lie.
Go kneel to him— for if he see thy face,
Or hear thy voice, he shall not doubt, but save.

LIEBHAID.   Never!   If I be offspring to that kite,
I here deny my race, forsake my father,—
So does thy dream fall true.   Let him save thee,
Whose hand has guided mine, whose lips have blessed,
Whose bread has nourished me.   Thy God is mine,
Thy people are my people.

VOICES (*without*).   Süsskind von Orb!

SUSSKIND.   I come, my friends.

(Enter boisterously certain Jews.)

1ST JEW.   Come to the house of God!

2D JEW.   Wilt thou desert us for whose sake we perish?

3D JEW.   The awful hour draws nigh.   Come forth with us
Unto the Synagogue.

SUSSKIND.   Bear with me, neighbors.
Here we may weep, here for the last time know
The luxury of sorrow, the soft touch
Of natural tenderness; here our hearts may break;
Yonder no tears, no faltering!   Eyes serene
Lifted to heaven, and defiant brows
To those who have usurped the name of men,
Must prove our faith and valor limitless
As is their cruelty.   One more embrace,
My daughter, thrice my daughter!   Thine affection
Outshines the hellish flames of hate; farewell,
But for a while; beyond the river of fire
I'll fold thee in mine arms, immortal angel!
For thee, poor orphan, soon to greet again
The blessed brows of parents, I dreamed not
The grave was all the home I had to give.
Go thou with Liebhaid, and array yourselves
As for a bridal.   Come, little son, with me.

Friends, I am ready. Oh, my God, my God,
Forsake us not in our extremity!

(Exeunt Süsskind and Jews.)

SCENE II.—A Street in the Judengasse. Several Jews pass across the stage, running
and with gestures of distress.

JEWS. Woe, woe! the curse has fallen! (*Exeunt*)

(Enter other Jews.)

1ST JEW. We are doomed.
The fury of the Lord has smitten us.
Oh that mine head were waters and mine eyes
Fountains of tears!* God has forsaken us.

(They knock at the doors of the houses.)

2D JEW. What, Benjamin! Open the door to death!
We all shall die at sunset! Menachem!
Come forth! Come forth! Manasseh! Daniel! Ezra!

(Jews appear at the windows.)

ONE CALLING FROM ABOVE. Neighbors, what wild alarm is this?
1ST JEW.   Descend!
Descend! Come with us to the house of prayer.
Save himself whoso can! we all shall burn.

(Men and women appear at the doors of the houses.)

ONE OF THE MEN AT THE DOOR. Beseech you brethren, calmly!
Tell us all!
Mine aged father lies at point of death
Gasping within. Ye'll thrust him in his grave
With boisterous clamor.
1ST JEW.   Blessed is the man
Whom the Lord calls unto Himself in peace!
Süsskind von Orb and Rabbi Jacob come
From the tribunal where the vote is—Death
To all our race.
SEVERAL VOICES. Woe! woe! God pity us!
1ST JEW. Hie ye within, and take a last farewell
Of home, love, life—put on your festal robes.
So wills the Rabbi, and come forth at once
To pray till sunset in the Synagogue.
AN OLD MAN. Oh God! Is this the portion of mine age?
Were my white hairs, my old bones spared for this?
Oh cruel, cruel!
A YOUNG GIRL.   I am too young to die.
Save me, my father! To-morrow should have been
The feast at Rachel's house. I longed for that,
Counted the days, dreaded some trivial chance
Might cross my pleasure —Lo, this horror comes!

---

* Jeremiah ix. 1.

A BRIDE.   Oh love! oh thou just-tasted cup of joy
Snatched from my lips!   Shall we twain lie with death,
Dark, silent, cold—whose every sense was tuned
To happiness!   Life was too beautiful—
That was the dream—how soon we are awake!
Ah, we have that within our hearts defies
Their fiercest flames.   No end, no end, no end!
JEW.   *God with a mighty hand, a stretched-out arm,
And poured-out fury, ruleth over us.
The sword is furbished, sharp i' the slayer's hand.
Cry out and howl thou son of Israel!
Thou shalt be fuel to the fire; thy blood
Shall overflow the land, and thou no more
Shalt be remembered—so the Lord hath spoken.
(Exeunt omnes.)

SCENE III.—Within the Synagogue.   Above in the Gallery, women sumptuously
attired; some with children by the hand or infants in their arms.   Below the men
and boys with silken scarfs about their shoulders.

RABBI JACOB.   †The Lord is nigh unto the broken heart.
Out of the depths we cry to thee, oh God !
Show us the path of everlasting life ;
For in thy presence is the plenitude
Of joy, and in thy right hand endless bliss.
(Enter Süsskind, Reuben, etc.)

SEVERAL VOICES.   Woe unto us who perish !
A JEW.   Süsskind von Orb,
Thou hast brought down this doom.   Would we had heard
The prophet's voice !
SUSSKIND.   Brethren, my cup is full !
Oh let us die as warriors of the Lord.
The Lord is great in Zion.   Let our death
Bring no reproach to Jacob, no rebuke
To Israel.   Hark ye ! let us crave one boon
At our assassins' hands ; beseech them build
Within God's acre where our fathers sleep,
A dancing-floor to hide the fagots stacked.
Then let the minstrels strike the harp and lute,
And we will dance and sing above the pile,
Fearless of death, until the flames engulf,
Even as David danced before the Lord,
As Miriam danced and sang beside the sea.
Great is our Lord ! His name is glorious
In Judah, and extolled in Israel !
In Salem is his tent, his dwelling place
In Zion ; let us chant the praise of God !
A JEW.   Süsskind, thou speakest well   We will meet death

---

* Ezekiel xx. 33; xxi. 11-32·
† Service for Day of Atonement.

With dance and song. Embrace him as a bride.
So that the Lord receive us in His tent.
SEVERAL VOICES. Amen! amen! amen! we dance to death!
RABBI JACOB. Süsskind, go forth and beg this grace of them.
(Exit Süsskind.)
Punish us not in wrath, chastise us not
In anger, oh our God! Our sins o'erwhelm
Our smitten heads, they are a grievous load ;
We look on our iniquities, we tremble,
Knowing our trespasses. Forsake us not.
Be thou not far from us. Haste to our aid,
Oh God, who art our Saviour and our Rock !
(Re-enter Süsskind.)
SUSSKIND. Brethren, our prayer, being the last, is granted.
The hour approaches. Let our thoughts ascend
From mortal anguish, to the ecstasy
Of martyrdom, the blessed death of those
Who perish in the Lord. I see, I see
How Israel's ever-crescent glory makes
These flames that would eclipse it, dark as blots
Of candlelight against the blazing sun.
We die a thousand deaths,—drown, bleed and burn;
Our ashes are dispersed unto the winds.
Yet the wild winds cherish the sacred seed,
The waters guard it in their crystal heart,
The fire refuseth to consume. It springs,
A tree immortal, shadowing many lands,
Unvisited, unnamed, undreamed as yet.
Rather a vine, full-flowered, golden-branched,
Ambrosial-fruited, creeping on the earth,
Trod by the passer's foot, yet chosen to deck
Tables of princes. Israel now has fallen
Into the depths, he shall be great in time.†
Even as we die in honor, from our death
Shall bloom a myriad heroic lives,
Brave through our bright example, virtuous
Lest our great memory fall in disrepute.
Is one among us, brothers, would exchange
His doom against our tyrants,—lot for lot ?
Let him go forth and live—he is no Jew.
Is one who would not die in Israel
Rather than live in Christ,—their Christ who smiles
On such a deed as this ? Let him go forth—
He may die full of years upon his bed.
Ye who nurse rancor haply in your hearts,
Fear ye we perish unavenged ? Not so !

† The vine creeps on the earth, trodden by the passer's foot, but its fruit goes up-
on the table of princes. Israel now has fallen in the depths, but he shall be great
in the fulness of time.—TALMUD.

To-day, no ! nor to-morrow ! but in God's time,
Our witnesses arise. Ours is the truth,
Ours is the power, the gift of Heaven. We hold
His Law, His lamp His covenant, His pledge,
Wherever in the ages shall arise
Jew-priest, Jew-poet, Jew-singer, or Jew-saint—
And everywhere I see them star the gloom—
In each of these the martyrs are avenged !

RABBI JACOB. Bring from the ark, the bell-fringed, silken-bound
Scrolls of the Law. Gather the silver vessels,
Dismantle the rich curtains of the doors,
Bring the perpetual lamp ; all these shall burn,
For Israel's light is darkened, Israel's Law
Profaned by strangers. Thus the Lord hath said :
"*The weapon formed against thee shall not prosper,
The tongue that shall contend with thee in judgment,
Thou shalt condemn. This is the heritage
Of the Lord's servants and their righteousness.
For thou shalt come to peoples yet unborn,
Declaring that which He hath done. Amen !"
(The doors of the Synagogue are burst open with tumultuous noise, Citizens and officers rush in.)

CITIZENS. Come forth ! the sun sets   Come, the Council waits !
What ! will ye teach your betters patience ? Out !
The Governor is ready. Forth with you,
Curs ! serpents ! Judases ! The bonfire burns !
[Exeunt]

SCENE IV.—A Public Place. Crowds of citizens assembled. On a platform are
seated DIETRICH VON TETTENBORN and HENRY SCHNETZEN with other members
of the Council.

1ST CITIZEN. Here's such a throng ! Neighbor, your elbow makes
An ill prod for my ribs.

2D CITIZEN.   I am pushed and squeezed.
My limbs are not mine own.

3D CITIZEN.   Look this way, wife.
They will come hence,—a pack of just-whipped curs.
I warrant you the stiff-necked brutes repent
To-day if ne'er before.

WIFE.   I am all a-quiver.
I have seen monstrous sights,—an uncaged wolf,
The corpse of one sucked by a vampyre,
The widow Kupfen's malformed child—but never
Until this hour, a Jew.

3D CITIZEN.   D'ye call me Jew ?
Where do you spy one now ?

WIFE   You'll have your jest
Now or anon, what matters it ?

4TH CITIZEN.   Well, I

_____
* Conclusion of service for Day of Atonement.

Have seen a Jew, and seen one burn at that;
Hard by in Wartburg; he had killed a child.
Zounds! how the serpent wriggled! I smell now
The roasting, stinking flesh!

BOY.   Father, be these
The folk who murdered Jesus?

4TH CITIZEN.   Ay, my boy.
Remember that, and when you hear them come,
I'll lift you on my shoulders. You can fling
Your pebbles with the rest.

(Trumpets sound.)

CITIZENS.   The Jews! the Jews!

BOY   Quick, father! lift me! I see nothing here
But hose and skirts.

(Music of a march approaching).

CITIZENS.   What mummery is this?
The sorcerers brew new mischief.

ANOTHER CITIZEN.   Why, they come
Pranked for a holiday: not veiled for death.

ANOTHER CITIZEN.   Insolent braggarts! They defy the Christ!

(Enter in procession to music the Jews. First RABBI JACOB—after him, sick people carried on litters—then old men and women, followed promiscuously by men, women and children of all ages. Some of the men carry gold and silver vessels, some the Rolls of the Law. One bears the Perpetual Lamp, another the seven-branched silver candle-stick of the Synagogue. The mothers have their children by the hand or in their arms. All richly attired.)

CITIZENS.   The misers! they will take their gems and gold
Down to the grave!

CITIZEN'S WIFE.   So these be Jews! Christ save us!
To think the devils look like human folk!

CITIZENS.   Cursed be the poison-mixers! Let them burn!

CITIZENS.   Burn! burn!

(Enter Süsskind von Orb, Liebhaid, Reuben and Claire.)

SCHNETZEN.   Good God! what maid is that?

TETTENBORN.   Liebhaid von Orb.

SCHNETZEN.   The devil's trick!
He has bewitched mine eyes.

SUSSKIND (as he passes the platform.)   Woe to the father
Who murders his own child!

SCHNETZEN.   I am avenged,
Süsskind von Orb! Blood for blood, fire for fire,
And death for death!

(Exeunt Süsskind, Liebhaid, etc.)
(Enter Jewish youths and maidens.)

YOUTHS (in chorus.)   Let us rejoice, for it is promised us
That we shall enter in God's tabernacle!

MAIDENS.   Our feet shall stand within thy gates, O Zion,
Within thy portals, O Jerusalem!

(Exeunt.)

CITIZEN'S WIFE. I can see naught from here. Let's follow, Hans.
CITIZEN. Be satisfied. There is no inch of space
For foot to rest on yonder. Look ! look there !
How the flames rise !
BOY. Oh father, I can see !
They all are dancing in the crimson blaze.
Look how their garments wave, their jewels shine,
When the smoke parts a bit. The tall flames dart.
Is not the fire real fire ? They fear it not.
VOICES WITHOUT. Arise, oh house of Jacob. Let us walk
Within the light of the Almighty Lord !

(Enter in furious haste Prince William and Nordmann.)

PRINCE W. Respite ! You kill your daughter, Henry Schnetzen !
NORDMANN. Liebhaid von Orb is your own flesh and blood,
SCHNETZEN. Spectre ! do dead men rise ?
NORDMANN. Yea, for revenge !
I swear, Lord Schnetzen, by my knightly honor,
She who is dancing yonder to her death,
Is thy wife's child !

(Schnetzen and Prince William make a rush forward towards the flames. Music
ceases; a sound of crashing boards is heard and a great cry—HALLELUJAH!

PRINCE W. AND SCHNETZEN. Too late ! too late !
CITIZENS. All's done !
PRINCE W. The fire ! the fire ! Liebhaid. I come to thee.

(He is about to spring forward but is held back by guards)

SCHNETZEN. Oh cruel Christ ! Is there no bolt in heaven
For the child murderer ? Kill me, my friends ! my breast
Is bare to all your swords.

(He tears open his jerkin and falls unconscious.)

(Curtain falls.)

THE END.

The plot and incidents of this Tragedy are taken from a little narrative entitled
" Der Tanz zum Tode; ein Nachtstück aus dem vierzehnten Yahrhundert," (The
Dance to Death—a Night-piece of the fourteenth century,). By Richard Reinhard.
Compiled from authentic documents communicated by Professor Franz Delitzsch.
The original narrative thus disposes in conclusion of the principal characters:—
"The Knight Henry Schnetzen ended his curse-stricken life in a cloister of the strict-
est order.
" Herr Nordmann was placed in close confinement, and during the same year his
head fell under the sword of the executioner.
"Prince William returned, broken down with sorrow, to Eisenach. His princely
father's heart found no comfort during the remainder of his days. He died soon
after the murder of the Jews—his last words were, 'woe! the fire!'
"William reached an advanced age, but his life was joyless. He never married,and
at his death Meissen was inherited by his nephew.
"The Jewish cemetery in Nordhausen, the scene of this martyrdom lay for a long
time waste. Nobody would build upon it. Now it is a bleaching meadow, and
where once the flames sprang up, to-day rests peaceful sunshine."

SONGS.

THE NEW YEAR.

ROSH-HASHANAH, 5643.

Not while the snow-shroud round dead earth is rolled,
　And naked branches point to frozen skies.—
When orchards burn their lamps of fiery gold,
　The grape glows like a jewel, and the corn
A sea of beauty and abundance lies,
　　　　Then the new year is born.

Look where the mother of the months uplifts
　In the green clearness of the unsunned West,
Her ivory horn of plenty, dropping gifts,
　Cool, harvest-feeding dews, fine-winnowed light;
Tired labor with fruition, joy and rest
　　　　Profusely to requite.

Blow, Israel, the sacred cornet! Call
　Back to thy courts whatever faint heart throb
With thine ancestral blood, thy need craves all.
　The red, dark year is dead, the year just born
Leads on from anguish wrought by priest and mob,
　　　　To what undreamed-of morn?

For never yet, since on the holy height,
　The Temple's marble walls of white and green
Carved like the sea-waves, fell, and the world's light
　Went out in darkness,—never was the year
Greater with portent and with promise seen,
　　　　Than this eve now and here.

Even as the Prophet promised, so your tent
　Hath been enlarged unto earth's farthest rim.
To snow-capped Sierras from vast steppes ye went,
　Through fire and blood and tempest-tossing wave,
For freedom to proclaim and worship Him,
　　　　Mighty to slay and save.

High above flood and fire ye held the scroll,
　Out of the depths ye published still the Word.
No bodily pang had power to swerve your soul :
　Ye, in a cynic age of crumbling faiths,
Lived to bear witness to the living Lord,
　　　　Or died a thousand deaths.

In two divided streams the exiles part,
　One rolling homeward to its ancient source,
One rushing sunward with fresh will, new heart.
　By each the truth is spread, the law unfurled,
Each separate soul contains the nation's force,
　　　　And both embrace the world.

Kindle the silver candle's seven rays,
  Offer the firstfruits of the clustered bowers,
The garnered spoil of bees. With prayer and praise
  Rejoice that once more tried, once more we prove
How strength of supreme suffering still is ours
        For Truth and Law and Love.

THE CROWING OF THE RED COCK.

Across the Eastern sky has glowed
  The flicker of a blood-red dawn
Once more the clarion cock has crowed,
  Once more the sword of Christ is drawn.
A million burning rooftrees light
The world-wide path of Israel's flight.

Where is the Hebrew's fatherland?
  The folk of Christ is sore bested ;
The Son of Man is bruised and banned,
  Nor finds whereon to lay his head.
His cup is gall, his meat is tears,
His passion lasts a thousand years.

Each crime that wakes in man the beast,
  Is visited upon his kind.
The lust of mobs, the greed of priest,
  The tyranny of kings, combined
To root his seed from earth again,
His record is one cry of pain.

When the long roll of Christian guilt
  Against his sires and kin is known,
The flood of tears, the life-blood spilt,
  The agony of ages shown,
What oceans can the stain remove,
From Christian law and Christian love?

Nay, close the book ; not now, not here,
  The hideous tale of sin narrate,
Reëchoing in the martyr's ear,
  Even he might nurse revengeful hate,
Even he might turn in wrath sublime,
With blood for blood and crime for crime.

Coward? Not he, who faces death,
  Who singly against worlds has fought,
For what? A name he may not breathe
  For liberty of prayer and thought.
The angry sword he will not whet,
His nobler task is—to forget.

IN EXILE.

"Since that day till now our life is one unbroken paradise. We live a true brotherly life. Every evening after supper we take a seat under the mighty oak and sing our songs.—*Extract from a letter of a Russian refugee in Texas.*

Twilight is here, soft breezes bow the grass,
　Day's sounds of various toil break slowly off.
The yoke-freed oxen low, the patient ass
　Dips his dry nostril in the cool, deep trough.
Up from the prairie the tanned herdsmen pass
　With frothy pails, guiding with voices rough
Their udder-lightened kine. Fresh smells of earth,
The rich, black furrows of the glebe send forth.

After the Southern day of heavy toil,
　How good to lie, with limbs relaxed, brows bare
To evening's fan, and watch the smoke-wreaths coil
　Up from one's pipe-stem through the rayless air.
So deem these unused tillers of the soil,
Who stretched beneath the shadowing oak tree, stare
Peacefully on the star-unfolding skies,
And name their life unbroken paradise.

The hounded stag that has escaped the pack,
　And pants at ease within a thick-leaved dell ;
The unimprisoned bird that finds the track
　Through sun-bathed space, to where his fellows dwell;
The martyr, granted respite from the rack,
　The death-doomed victim pardoned from his cell,—
Such only know the joy these exiles gain,—
Life's sharpest rapture is surcease of pain.

Strange faces theirs, wherethrough the Orient sun
　Gleams from the eyes and glows athwart the skin.
Grave lines of studious thought and purpose run
　From curl-crowned forehead to dark-bearded chin.
And over all the seal is stamped thereon
　Of anguish branded by a world of sin,
In fire and blood through ages on their name,
Their seal of glory and the Gentiles' shame.

Freedom to love the law that Moses brought,
　To sing the songs of David, and to think
The thoughts Gabirol to Spinoza taught,
　Freedom to dig the common earth, to drink
The universal air—for this they sought
　Refuge o'er wave and continent, to link
Egypt with Texas in their mystic chain,
And truth's perpetual lamp forbid to wane.

Hark ! through the quiet evening air, their song
    Floats forth with wild, sweet rhythm and glad refrain.
They sing the conquest of the spirit strong,
    The soul that wrests the victory from pain ;
The noble joys of manhood that belong
    To comrades and to brothers.   In their strain
Rustle of palms and Eastern streams one hears.
And the broad prairie melts in mist of tears.

IN MEMORIAM—REV. J. J. LYONS.

ROSH-HASHANAH, 5638.

The golden harvest-tide is here, the corn
Bows its proud tops beneath the reaper's hand.
Ripe orchards' plenteous yields enrich the land;
Bring the first fruits and offer them this morn,
With the stored sweetness of all summer hours,
The amber honey sucked from myriad flowers,
And sacrifice your best, first fruits to-day,
With fainting hearts and hands forespent with toil,
Offer the mellow harvest's splendid spoil,
To Him who gives and Him who takes away.

Bring timbrels, bring the harp of sweet accord,
And in a pleasant psalm your voice attune,
And blow the cornet greeting the new moon.
Sing, holy, holy, holy, is the Lord,
Who killeth and who quickeneth again,
Who woundeth, and who healeth mortal pain,
Whose hand afflicts us, and who sends us peace.
Hail thou slim arc of promise in the West,
Thou pledge of certain plenty, peace, and rest.
With the spent year, may the year's sorrows cease.

For there is mourning now in Israel,
The crown, the garland of the branching tree
Is plucked and withered   Ripe of years was he.
The priest, the good old man who wrought so well
Upon his chosen glebe.   For he was one
Who at his seed-plot toiled through rain and sun.
Morn found him not as one who slumbereth,
Noon saw him faithful, and the restful night
Stole o'er him at his labors to requite
The just man's service with the just man's death.

What shall be said when such as he do pass?
Go to the hill-side, neath the cypress-trees,
Fall midst that peopled silence on your knees,

And weep that man must wither as the grass.
But mourn him not, whose blameless life complete
Rounded its perfect orb, whose sleep is sweet,
Whom we must follow, but may not recall.
Salute with solemn trumpets the New Year,
And offer honeyed fruits as were he here,
Though ye be sick with wormwood and with gall.

THE VALLEY OF BACA.

PSALM LXXXIV.

A brackish lake is there with bitter pools
  Anigh its margin, brushed by heavy trees.
A piping wind the narrow valley cools,
  Fretting the willows and the cypresses.
Gray skies above, and in the gloomy space
An awful presence hath its dwelling-place.

I saw a youth pass down that vale of tears;
  His head was circled with a crown of thorn,
His form was bowed as by the weight of years,
  His wayworn feet by stones were cut and torn.
His eyes were such as have beheld the sword
Of terror of the angel of the Lord.

He passed, and clouds and shadows and thick haze
  Fell and encompassed him   I might not see
What hand upheld him in those dismal ways,
  Wherethrough he staggered with his misery.
The creeping mists that trooped and spread around,
The smitten head and writhing form enwound.

Then slow and gradual but sure they rose,
  Those clinging vapors blotting out the sky.
The youth had fallen not, his viewless foes
  Discomfited, had left the victory
Unto the heart that fainted not nor failed,
But from the hill tops its salvation hailed.

I looked at him in dread lest I should see,
  The anguish of the struggle in his eyes;
And lo, great peace was there! Triumphantly
  The sunshine crowned him from the sacred skies.
"From strength to strength he goes," he leaves beneath
The valley of the shadow and of death.

  " Thrice blest who passing through that vale of Tears,
    Makes it a well,"—and draws life-nourishment

From those death-bitter drops.   No grief, no fears
  Assail him further, he may scorn the event.
For naught hath power to swerve the steadfast soul
Within that valley broken and made whole.

THE BANNER OF THE JEW.

Wake, Israel, wake! Recall to-day
  The glorious Maccabean rage,
The sire heroic, hoary-gray,
  His five-fold lion-lineage:
The Wise, the Elect, the Help-of-God,
  The Burst-of-Spring, the Avenging Rod. *

From Mizpeh's mountain-ridge they saw
  Jerusalem's empty streets, her shrine
Laid waste where Greeks profaned the Law,
  With idol and with pagan sign.
Mourners in tattered black were there,
  With ashes sprinkled on their hair.

Then from the stony peak there rang
  A blast to ope the graves : down poured
The Maccabean clan, who sang
  Their battle-anthem to the Lord.
Five heroes lead, and following, see,
  Ten thousand rush to victory '

Oh for Jerusalem's trumpet now,
  To blow a blast of shattering power,
To wake the sleepers high and low,
  And rouse them to the urgent hour !
No hand for vengeance—but to save,
  A million naked swords should wave.

Oh deem not dead that martial fire,
  Say not the mystic flame is spent !
With Moses' law and David's lyre,
  Your ancient strength remains unbent.
Let but an Ezra rise anew,
  To lift the *Banner of the Jew !*

A rag, a mock at first—erelong,
  When men have bled and women wept,
To guard its precious folds from wrong,
  Even they who shrunk, even they who slept,
Shall leap to bless it, and to save.
  Strike ! for the brave revere the brave !

---

* The sons of Mattathias—Jonathan, John, Eleazar, Simon
(also called the Jewel), and Judas, the Prince.

THE GUARDIAN OF THE RED DISK.

SPOKEN BY A CITIZEN OF MALTA—1300.

A curious title held in high repute,
One among many honors, thickly strewn
On my lord Bishop's head, his grace of Malta.
Nobly he bears them all,—with tact, skill, zeal,
Fulfills each special office, vast or slight,
Nor slurs the least minutia,—therewithal
Wears such a stately aspect of command,
Broad cheeked, broad-chested, reverend, sanctified,
Haloed with white about the tonsure's rim,
With dropped lids o'er the piercing Spanish eyes
(Lynx-keen, I warrant, to spy out heresy);
Tall, massive form, o'ertowering all in presence,
Or ere they kneel to kiss the large white hand.
His looks sustain his deeds,—the perfect prelate,
Whose void chair shall be taken, but not filled.

You know not, who are foreign to the isle,
Haply, what this Red Disk may be, he guards.
'Tis the bright blotch, big as the Royal seal,
Branded beneath the beard of every Jew.
These vermin so infest the isle, so slide
Into all byways, highways that may lead
Direct or roundabout to wealth or power,
Some plain, plump mark was needed, to protect
From the degrading contact Christian folk.

The evil had grown monstrous: certain Jews
Wore such a haughty air, had so refined,
With super-subtile arts, strict, monkish lives,
And studious habit, the coarse Hebrew type,
One might have elbowed in the public mart
Iscariot,—nor suspected one's soul-peril.
Christ's blood! it sets my flesh a creep to think!
We may breathe freely now, not fearing taint,
Praised be our good Lord Bishop! He keeps count
Of every Jew, and prints on cheek or chin
The scarlet stamp of separateness, of shame.

No beard, blue-black, grizzled or Judas-colored,
May hide that damning little wafer-flame.
When one appears therewith, the urchins know
Good sport's at hand; they fling their stones and mud,
Sure of their game. But most the wisdom shows
Upon the unbelievers' selves; they learn

Their proper rank; crouch, cringe and hide,—lay by
Their insolence of self-esteem; no more
Flaunt forth in rich attire, but in dull weeds,
Slovenly donned, would slink past unobserved;
Bow servile necks and crook obsequious knees,
Chin sunk in hollow chest, eyes fixed on earth
Or blinking sidewise, but to apprehend
Whether or not the hated spot be spied.
I warrant my lord Bishop has full hands,
Guarding the Red Disk—lest one rogue escape!

A TRANSLATION AND TWO IMITATIONS.

I.

DONNA CLARA.

(FROM THE GERMAN OF HEINE).

In the evening through her garden
    Wanders the Alcalde's daughter,
Festal sounds of drum and trumpet
    Ring out hither from the Castle.

"I am weary of the dances,
    Honeyed word of adulation
From the knights who still compare me
    To the sun with dainty phrases.

Yes, of all things I am weary,
    Since I first beheld by moonlight
Him, my cavalier, whose zither
    Nightly draws me to my casement.

As he stands so slim and daring,
    With his flaming eyes that sparkle,
And with nobly pallid features
    Truly, he St. George resembles."

Thus went Donna Clara dreaming,
    On the ground her eyes were fastened.
When she raised them, lo! before her
    Stood the handsome knightly stranger.

Pressing hands and whispering passion,
    These twain wander in the moonlight,
Gently doth the breeze caress them,
    The enchanted roses greet them.

The enchanted roses greet them,
  And they glow like Love's own heralds.
" Tell me, tell me, my beloved,
  Wherefore all at once thou blushest ? "

" Gnats were stinging me, my darling,
  And I hate these gnats in summer
E'en as though they were a rabble
  Of vile Jews with long, hooked noses."

" Heed not gnats nor Jews, beloved,"
  Spake the knight with fond endearments.
From the almond trees dropped downward
  Myriad snowy flakes of blossoms.

Myriad snowy flakes of blossoms
  Shed around them fragrant odors.
" Tell me, tell me, my beloved,
  Looks thy heart on me with favor ? "

" Yes, I love thee, O my darling,
  And I swear it by our Savior,
Whom the accursed Jews did murder,
  Long ago with wicked malice."

" Heed thou neither Jews nor Savior,"
  Spake the knight with fond endearments.
Far off waved as in a vision,
  Gleaming lilies bathed in moonlight.

Gleaming lilies bathed in moonlight
  Seemed to watch the stars above them.
" Tell, me, tell me, my beloved,
  Didst thou not erewhile swear falsely ? "

" Naught is false in me, my darling,
  E'en as in my veins there floweth
Not a drop of blood that's Moorish,.
  Neither of foul Jewish current."

" Heed not Moors nor Jews, beloved,"
  Spake the knight with fond endearments.
Then towards a grove of myrtles
  Leads he the Alcalde's daughter.

And with Love's slight subtile meshes,
  He has trapped her and entangled.
Brief their words, but long their kisses,
  For their hearts are overflowing.

What a melting bridal carol
  Sings the nightingale, the pure one.
How the fire-flies in the grasses
  Trip their sparkling torchlight dances !

In the grove the silence deepens,
   Naught is heard save furtive rustling
Of the swaying myrtle branches,
   And the breathing of the flowers.

But the sound of drum and trumpet
   Burst forth sudden from the castle.
Rudely they awaken Clara,
   Pillowed on her Lover's bosom.

"Hark! they summon me, my darling!
   But before we part, oh tell me,
Tell me what thy precious name is,
   Which so closely thou hast hidden."

Then the knight with gentle laughter,
   Kissed the fingers of his Donna,
Kissed her lips and kissed her forehead,
   And at last these words he uttered:

"I, Senora, your beloved,
   Am the son of the respected,
Worthy, erudite Grand Rabbi,
   Israel of Saragossa."

(The *ensemble* of the romance is a scene of my own life—only the Park of Berlin has become the Alcalde's garden, the Baroness a Senora, and myself a St. George or even an Apollo. This was only to be the first part of a trilogy, the second of which shows the hero jeered at by his own child who does not know him, whilst the third discovers this child who has become a Dominican, and is torturing to the death his Jewish brethren. The refrain of these two pieces corresponds with that of the first. Indeed this little poem was not intended to excite laughter, still less to denote a mocking spirit. I merely wished without any definite purpose to render with epic impartiality in this poem an individual circumstance, and at the same time something general and universal—a moment in the world's history which was distinctly reflected in my experience, and I had conceived the whole idea in a spirit which was anything rather than smiling, but serious and painful, so much so, that it was to form the first part of a tragic trilogy.

HEINE'S CORRESPONDENCE.

Guided by these hints, I have endeavored to carry out in the two following original Ballads the Poet's first conception.

EMMA LAZARUS.)

II.

DON PEDRILLO.

Not a lad in Saragossa
   Nobler-featured, haughtier-tempered,
Then the Alcalde's youthful grandson,
   Donna Clara's boy Pedrillo.

Handsome as the Prince of Evil,
   And devout as St. Ignatius.
Deft at fence, unmatched with zither,
   Miniature of knightly virtues

Truly an unfailing blessing,
   To his pious, widowed mother.
To the beautiful, lone matron
   Who forswore the world to rear him.

For her beauty hath but ripened
   In such wise as the pomegranate
Putteth by her crown of blossoms,
   For her richer crown of fruitage.

Still her hand is claimed and courted,
   Still she spurns her proudest suitors,
Doting on a phantom passion,
   And upon her boy Pedrillo.

Like a saint lives Donna Clara,
   First at matins, last at vespers,
Half her fortune she expendeth
   Buying masses for the needy.

Visiting the poor afflicted,
   Infinite is her compassion,
Scorning not the Moorish beggar,
   Nor the wretched Jew despising.

And—a scandal to the faithful,
   E'en she hath been known to welcome
To her castle the young Rabbi,
   Offering to his tribe her bounty.

Rarely hath he crossed the threshold,
   Yet the thought that he hath crossed it,
Burns like poison in the marrow
   Of the zealous youth Pedrillo.

By the blessed Saint Iago,
   He hath vowed immortal hatred
To these circumcised intruders
   Who pollute the soil of Spaniards.

Seated in his mother's garden,
　At high noon the boy Pedrillo
Playeth with his favorite parrot,
　Golden-green with streaks of scarlet.

" Pretty Dodo, speak thy lesson,"
　Coaxed Pedrillo—"thief and traitor"—
" Thief and traitor "—croaked the parrot,
　"Is the yellow-skirted Rabbi."

And the boy with peals of laughter,
　Stroked his favorite's head of emerald,
Raised his eyes, and lo! before him
　Stood the yellow-skirted Rabbi.

In his dark eyes gleamed no anger,
　No hot flush o'erspread his features.
'Neath his beard his pale lips quivered,
　And a shadow crossed his forehead.

Very gentle was his aspect,
　And his voice was mild and friendly,
" Evil words, my son, thou speakest,
　Teaching to the fowls of heaven.

" In our Talmud it stands written,
　Thrice curst is the tongue of slander,
Poisoning also with its victim,
　Him who speaks and him who listens."

But no whit abashed, Pedrillo,
　" What care I for curse of Talmud?
'Tis no slander to speak evil
　Of the murderers of our Savior.

" To your beard I will repeat it,
　That I only bide my manhood,
To wreak all my lawful hatred,
　On thyself and on thy people."

Very gently spoke the Rabbi,
　"Have a care, my son Pedrillo,
Thou art orphaned, and who knoweth,
　But thy father loved this people?"

" Think you words like these will touch me?
　Such I laugh to scorn, sir Rabbi,
From high heaven, my sainted father
　On my deeds will smile in blessing.

" Loyal knight was he and noble,
　And my mother oft assures me,
Ne'er she saw so pure a Christian,
　'Tis from him my zeal deriveth."

"What if he were such another
  As myself who stand before thee?"
" I should curse the hour that bore me,
  I should die of shame and horror."

" Harsher is thy creed than ours;
  For had I a son as comely
As Pedrillo, I would love him,
  Love him were he thrice a Christian.

" In his youth my youth renewing
  Pamper, fondle, die to serve him,
Only breathing through his spirit—
  Couldst thou not love such a father?"

Faltering spoke the deep-voiced Rabbi,
  With white lips and twitching fingers,
Then in clear, young, steady treble,
  Answered him the boy Pedrillo:

" At the thought my heart revolteth,
  All your tribe offend my senses,
They're an eyesore to my vision,
  And a stench unto my nostrils.

" When I meet these unbelievers,
  With thick lips and eagle noses,
Thus I scorn them, thus revile them,
  Thus I spit upon their garment."

And the haughty youth passed onward,
  Bearing on his wrist his parrot,
And the yellow skirted Rabbi
  With bowed head sought Donna Clara.

III.

FRA PEDRO.

Golden lights and lengthening shadows,
  Flings the splendid sun declining,
O'er the monastery garden
  Rich in flower, fruit and foliage.

Through the avenue of nut trees,
  Pace two grave and ghostly friars,
Snowy white their gowns and girdles,
  Black as night their cowls and mantles.

Lithe and ferret–eyed the younger,
  Black his scapular denoting
A lay brother; his companion
  Large. imperious, towers above him.

'Tis the abbot, great Fra Pedro,
  Famous through all Saragossa,
For his quenchless zeal in crushing
  Heresy amidst his townfolk.

Handsome still with hood and tonsure,
  E'en as when the boy Pedrillo,
Insolent with youth and beauty,
  Who reviled the gentle Rabbi.

Lo, the level sun strikes sparkles,
  From his dark eyes brightly flashing,
Stern his voice: " These too shall perish.
  I have vowed extermination.

" Tell not me of skill or virtue,
  Filial love or woman's beauty.
Jews are Jews, as serpents serpents,
  In themselves abomination."

Earnestly the other pleaded,
  " If my zeal, thrice reverend master,
E'er afforded thee assistance.
  Serving thee as flesh serves spirit.

" Hounding, scourging, flaying, burning,
  Casting into chains or exile,
At thy bidding these vile wretches,
  Hear and heed me now, my master.

"These be nowise like their brethren,
  Ben Jehudah is accounted
Saragossa's first physician,
Loved by colleague as by patient.

" And his daughter Donna Zara
  Is our city's pearl of beauty,
Like the clusters of the vineyard,
  Droop the ringlets o'er her temples

" Like the moon in starry heavens,
  Shines her face among her people,
And her form hath all the languor,
  Grace and glamour of the palm tree.

"Well thou knowest, thrice reverend master,
  This is not their first affliction,
Was it not our holy office,
  Whose bribed menials fired their dwelling?

" Ere dawn broke, the smoke ascended,
  Choked the stairways, filled the chambers,
Waked the household to the terror
  Of the flaming death that threatened.

" Then the poor bed ridden mother
  Knew her hour had come; two daughters,
Twinned in form, and mind, and spirit,
  And their father—who would save them?

" Towards her door sprang Ben Jehudah,
  Donna Zara flew behind him
Round his neck her white arms wreathing,
  Drew him from the burning chamber.

" There within, her sister Zillah
  Stirred no limb to shun her torture,
Held her mother's hand and kissed her,
  Saying, ' We will go together.'

"This the outer throng could witness,
  As the flames enwound the dwelling,
Like a glory they illumined
  Awfully the martyred daughter.

" Closer, fiercer, round they gathered,
  Not a natural cry escaped her,
Helpless clung to her her mother,
  Hand in hand they went together.

" Since that ' Act of Faith ' three winters
  Have rolled by, yet on the forehead
Of Jehudah is imprinted
  Still the horror of that morning.

" Saragossa hath respected
  His false creed; a man of sorrows,
He hath walked secure among us,
  And his art repays our sufferance."

Thus he spoke and ceased. The Abbot
  Lent him an impatient hearing,
Then outbroke with angry accent,
  " We have borne three years, thou sayest?

" ' Tis enough; my vow is sacred.
  These shall perish with their brethren.
Hark ye! In my veins' pure current
  Were a single drop found Jewish,

" I would shrink not from outpouring
  All my life blood, but to purge it.
Shall I gentler prove to others?
  Mercy would be sacrilegious.

" Ne'er again at thy soul's peril,
  Speak to me of Jewish beauty,
Jewish skill, or Jewish virtue.
  I have said.—Do thou remember."

Down behind the purple hillside
  Dropped the sun; above the garden
Rang the Angelus' clear cadence
  Summoning the monks to vespers.

TRANSLATIONS FROM THE HEBREW POETS

OF MEDIÆVAL SPAIN.

I

SOLOMON BEN JUDAH GABIROL.

(DIED BETWEEN 1070–80.)

Am I sipping the honey of the lips?
Am I drunk with the wine of a kiss?
Have I culled the flowers of the cheek,
Have I sucked the fresh fragrance of the breath?
Nay, it is the Song of Gabirol that has revived me,
The perfume of his youthful, spring-tide breeze."

MOSES BEN ESRA.

" I will engrave my songs indelibly upon the heart of the world,
so that no one can efface tnem."

GABIROL.

NIGHT-THOUGHTS.

Will night already spread her wings and weave
Her dusky robe about the day's bright form,
Boldly the sun's fair countenance displacing,
And swathe it with her shadow in broad day?
So a green wreath of mist enrings the moon,
Till envious clouds do quite encompass her.
No wind! and yet the slender stem is stirred,
With faint, slight motion as from inward tremor.
Mine eyes are full of grief—who sees me, asks,
"Oh wherefore dost thou cling unto the ground?"
My friends discourse with sweet and soothing words;
They all are vain, they glide above my head.
I fain would check my tears; would fain enlarge
Unto infinity, my heart—in vain!
Grief presses hard my breast, therefore my tears
Have scarcely dried, ere they again spring forth.
For these are streams, no furnace heat may quench,
Nebuchadnezzar's flames may dry them not.
What is the pleasure of the day for me,
If, in its crucible, I must renew
Incessantly the pangs of purifying?
Up, challenge, wrestle, and o'ercome! Be strong!

The late grapes cover all the vine with fruit.
I am not glad, though even the lion's pride
Content itself upon the field's poor grass.
My spirit sinks beneath the tide, soars not
With fluttering seamews on the moist, soft strand.
I follow fortune not, where'er she lead.
Lord o'er myself, I banish her, compel
And though her clouds should rain no blessed dew,
Though she withhold the crown, the heart's desire,
Though all deceive, though honey change to gall,
Still am I lord, and will in freedom strive.

MEDITATIONS.

Forget thine anguish,
   Vexed heart, again.
Why shouldst thou languish,
   With earthly pain?
The husk shall slumber,
   Bedded in clay
Silent and sombre,
   Oblivion's prey!
But, Spirit immortal,
Thou at Death's portal,
   Tremblest with fear.
   If he caress thee,
   Curse thee or bless thee,
   Thou must draw near,
From him the worth of thy works to hear.

   Why full of terror,
   Compassed with error,
   Trouble thy heart,
   For thy mortal part?
   The soul flies home—
   The corpse is dumb.
   Of all thou didst have,
Follows naught to the grave.
   Thou fliest thy nest,
Swift as a bird to thy place of rest.

   What avail grief and fasting,
   Where nothing is lasting?
   Pomp, domination,
   Become tribulation.
   In a health-giving draught,
   A death-dealing shaft.
   Wealth—an illusion,
   Power—a lie,

Over all, dissolution
Creeps silent and sly.
Unto others remain
The goods thou didst gain
With infinite pain,

Life is a vine-branch;
  A vintager, death.
He threatens and lowers
  More near with each breath.
Then hasten, arise!
  Seek God, oh my soul!
For time quickly flies,
  Still far is the goal.
Vain heart praying dumbly,
  Learn to prize humbly,
  The meanest of fare.
Forget all thy sorrow,
  Behold, Death is there!

  Dove-like lamenting,
  Be full of repenting,
Lift vision supernal
To raptures eternal.
  On ev'ry occasion
  Seek lasting salvation.
Pour thy heart out in weeping,
While others are sleeping.
Pray to Him when all's still,
Performing His will.
And so shall the angel of peace be thy warden,
And guide thee at last to the heavenly garden.

HYMN

Almighty! what is man?
  But flesh and blood.
Like shadows flee his days,
He marks not how they vanish from his gaze,
  Suddenly, he must die—
He droppeth, stunned, into nonentity.

  Almighty! what is man?
  A body frail and weak,
  Full of deceit and lies,
  Of vile hypocrisies.
Now like a flower blowing,
Now scorched by sunbeams glowing.
And wilt thou of his trespasses inquire?
  How may he ever bear

Thine anger just, thy vengeance dire?
  Punish him not, but spare,
For he is void of power and strength !

Almighty! what is man?
  By filthy lust possessed,
Whirled in a round of lies,
  Fond frenzy swells his breast.
The pure man sinks in mire and slime,
The noble shrinketh not from crime,
Wilt thou resent on him the charms of sin?
  Like fading grass,
  So shall he pass.
  Like chaff that blows
  Where the wind goes.
Then spare him, be thou merciful, O King,
Upon the dreaded day of reckoning!

  Almighty! what is man?
  The haughty son of time
  Drinks deep of sin,
And feeds on crime
Seething like waves that roll,
Hot as a glowing coal.
And wilt thou punish him for sins inborn?
  Lost and forlorn,
Then like the weakling he must fall,
Who some great hero strives withal.
Oh, spare him, therefore! let him win
  Grace for his sin!

  Almighty! what is man?
  Spotted in guilty wise,
  A stranger unto faith,
  Whose tongue is stained with lies,
And shalt thou count his sins—so is he lost,
  Uprooted by thy breath.
Like to a stream by tempest tossed.
His life falls from him like a cloak,
He passes into nothingness, like smoke.
Then spare him, punish not, be kind, I pray,
To him who dwelleth in the dust, an image wrought in clay!

  Almighty! what is man?
  A withered bough!
When he is awestruck by approaching doom.
Like a dried blade of grass, so weak, so low
The pleasure of his life is changed to gloom.
He crumbles like a garment spoiled with moth;

According to his sins wilt thou be wroth?
He melts like wax before the candle's breath,
Yea, like thin water, so he vanisheth,
Oh, spare him therefore, for thy gracious name,
And be not too severe upon his shame!

Almighty! what is man?
A faded leaf!
If thou dost weigh him in the balance—lo!
He disappears—a breath that thou dost blow.
His heart is ever filled
With lust of lies unstilled.
Wilt bear in mind his crime
Unto all time?
He fades away like clouds sun-kissed,
Dissolves like mist.
Then spare him! let him love and mercy win,
According to thy grace, and not according to his sin!

TO A DETRACTOR.

The Autumn promised, and he keeps
His word unto the meadow-rose.
The pure, bright ligntnings herald Spring,
Serene and glad the fresh earth shows.
The rain has quenched her children's thirst,
Her cheeks, but now so cold and dry,
Are soft and fair, a laughing face;
With clouds of purple shines the sky,
Though filled with light, yet veiled with haze.
Hark! hark! the turtle's mocking note
Outsings the valley-pigeon's lays.
Her wings are gemmed, and from her throat,
When the clear sun gleams back again,
It seems to me as though she wore
About her neck a jeweled chain.
Say, wilt thou darken such a light,
Wilt drag the clouds from heaven's height?
Although thy heart with anger swell,
Yet firm as marble, mine doth dwell.
Therein no fear thy wrath begets.
It is not shaken by thy threats.
Yea, hurl thy darts, thy weapons wield,
The strength of youth is still my shield.
My winged steed toward the heights doth bound,
The dust whirls upward from the ground;
My song is scanty, dost thou deem
Thine eloquence a mighty stream?
Only the blameless offering,

Not the profusion man may bring,
Prevaileth with our Lord and King.
The long days out of minutes grow,
And out of months the years arise,
Wilt thou be master of the wise,
Then learn the hidden stream to know,
That from the inmost heart doth flow.

FRAGMENT.

My friend spoke with insinuating tongue:
    " Drink wine, and thy flesh shall be made whole.
    Look how it hisses in the leathern bottle like a
    captured serpent."
Oh fool! can the sun be forged into a cask stopped
with earthly bungs. I know not that the power
of wine has ever overmastered my sorrows; for
these mighty giants I have found as yet no resting-
place.

STANZAS.

" With tears thy grief thou dost bemoan,
Tears that would melt the hardest stone,
Oh, wherefore sing'st thou not the vine?
Why chant'st thou not the praise of wine?
It chases pain with cunning art,
The craven slinks from out thy heart."

But I: Poor fools the wine may cheat,
Lull them with lying visions sweet.
Upon the wings of storm may bear
The heavy burden of their care.
The father's heart may harden so,
He feeleth not his own child's woe.

No ocean is the cup, no sea,
To drown my broad, deep misery.
It grows so rank, you cut it all,
The aftermath springs just as tall.
My heart and flesh are worn away,
Mine eyes are darkened from the day.

The lovely morning-red behold
Wave to the breeze her flag of gold.
The hosts of stars above the world,
Like banners vanishing are furled.
The dew shines bright; I bide forlorn,
And shudder with the chill of morn.

WINE AND GRIEF

With heavy groans did I approach my friends,
Heavy as though the mountains I would move.
The flagon they were murdering; they poured
Into the cup, wild-eyed, the grape's red blood.
No, they killed not, they breathed new life therein.
Then, too, in fiery rapture, burned my veins,
But soon the fumes had fled.   In vain, in vain!
Ye cannot fill the breach of the rent heart.
Ye crave a sensuous joy; ye strive in vain
To cheat with flames of passion, my despair.
So when the sinking sun draws near to night,
The sky's bright cheeks fade 'neath those tresses black.
Ye laugh—but silently the soul weeps on;
Ye cannot stifle her sincere lament.

DEFIANCE.

" Conquer the gloomy night of thy sorrow, for the
    morning greets thee with laughter.
Rise and clothe thyself with noble pride
Break loose from the tyranny of grief.
Thou standest alone among men,
Thy song is like a pearl in beauty."

So spake my friend.   'Tis well !
The billows of the stormy sea which overwhelmed my
    soul,—
These I subdue ; I quake not
Before the bow and arrow of destiny.
I endured with patience when he deceitfully lied to me
With his treacherous smile.

Yea, boldly I defy Fate,
I cringe not to envious Fortune.
I mock the towering floods.
My brave heart does not shrink—
This heart of mine, that, albeit young in years,
Is none the less rich in deep, keen-eyed experience.

A DEGENERATE AGE.

Where is the man who has been tried and found strong
    and sound ?
Where is the friend of reason and of knowledge ?
I see only sceptics and weaklings.
I see only prisoners in the durance of the senses.
And every fool and every spendthrift
Thinks himself as great a master as Aristotle.

Think'st thou that they have written poems ?
Call'st thou that a Song ?
I call it the cackling of ravens.
The zeal of the prophet must free poesy
From the embrace of wanton youths.
My song I have inscribed on the forehead of Time,
They know and hate it—for it is lofty.

II.

ABUL HASSAN JUDAH BEN HA-LEVI.

(BORN BETWEEN 1080–90.)

LOVE-SONG.

" See'st thou o'er my shoulders falling,
    Snake-like ringlets waving free ?
Have no fear, for they are twisted
    To allure thee unto me."

Thus she spake, the gentle dove,
    Listen to thy plighted love :—
" Ah, how long I wait, until
    Sweetheart cometh back (she said)
Laying his caressing hand
    Underneath my burning head."

SEPARATION.

And so we twain must part! Oh linger yet,
    Let me still feed my glance upon thine eyes.
Forget not, love, the days of our delight,
    And I our nights of bliss shall ever prize.
In dreams thy shadowy image I shall see,
    Oh even in my dream be kind to me !

Though I were dead, I none the less would hear
    Thy step, thy garment rustling on the sand.
And if thou waft me greetings from the grave,
    I shall drink deep the breath of that cold land.
Take thou my days, command this life of mine,
    If it can lengthen out the space of thine.

No voice I hear from lips death-pale and chill,
    Yet deep within my heart it echoes still.
My frame remains—my soul to thee yearns forth.
    A shadow I must tarry still on earth.
Back to the body dwelling here in pain,
    Return, my soul, make haste and come again !

LONGING FOR JERUSALEM.

Oh, city of the world, with sacred splendor blest,
My spirit yearns to thee from out the far-off West,
A stream of love wells forth when I recall thy day,
Now is thy temple waste, thy glory passed away.
Had I an eagle's wings, straight would I fly to thee,
Moisten thy holy dust with wet cheeks streaming free.
Oh, how I long for thee! albeit thy King has gone,
Albeit where balm once flowed, the serpent dwells alone.
Could I but kiss thy dust, so would I fain expire,
As sweet as honey then, my passion, my desire!

ON THE VOYAGE TO JERUSALEM.

I.

My two-score years and ten are over,
    Never again shall youth be mine.
The years are ready-winged for flying,
    What crav'st thou still of feast and wine?
Wilt thou still court man's acclamation,
    Forgetting what the Lord hath said?
And forfeiting thy weal eternal,
    By thine own guilty heart misled?
Shalt thou have never done with folly,
    Still fresh and new must it arise?
Oh heed it not, heed not the senses,
    But follow God, be meek and wise;
Yea, profit by thy days remaining,
    They hurry swiftly to the goal.
Be zealous in the Lord's high service,
    And banish falsehood from thy soul.
Use all thy strength, use all thy fervor,
    Defy thine own desires, awaken!
Be not afraid when seas are foaming,
    And earth to her foundations shaken.
Benumbed the hand then of the sailor,
    The captain's skill and power are lamed.
Gaily they sailed with colors flying,
    And now turn home again ashamed.
The ocean is our only refuge,
    The sandbank is our only goal,
The masts are swaying as with terror,
    And quivering does the vessel roll.
The mad wind frolics with the billows,
    Now smooths them low, now lashes high.
Now they are storming up like lions,
    And now like serpents sleek they lie;

And wave on wave is ever pressing,
 They hiss, they whisper, soft of tone.
Alack ! was that the vessel splitting ?
 Are sail and mast and rudder gone ?
Here, screams of fright, there, silent weeping,
 The bravest feels his courage fail.
What stead our prudence or our wisdo m?
 The soul itself can naught avail.
And each one to his God is crying,
 Soar up, my soul, to Him aspire,
Who wrought a miracle for Jordan,
 Extol Him, oh angelic choir !
Remember Him who stays the tempest,
 The stormy billows doth control,
Who quickeneth the lifeless body,
 And fills the empty frame with soul.
Behold ! once more appears a wonder,
 The angry waves erst raging wild,
Like quiet flocks of sheep reposing,
 So soft, so still, so gently mild.
The sun descends, and high in heaven,
 The golden-circled moon doth stand.
Within the sea the stars are straying,
 Like wanderers in an unknown land.
The lights celestial in the waters
 Are flaming clearly as above,
As though the very heavens descended,
 To seal a covenant of love.
Perchance both sea and sky, twin oceans,
 From the same source of grace are sprung.
'Twixt these my heart, a third sea, surges,
 With songs resounding, clearly sung.

II.

A watery waste the sinful world has grown,
With no dry spot whereon the eye can rest,
No man, no beast, no bird to gaze upon,
Can all be dead, with silent sleep possessed ?
Oh, how I long the hills and vales to see,
To find myself on barren steppes were bliss.
I peer about, but nothing greeteth me,
Naught save the ship, the clouds, the waves' abyss,
The crocodile which rushes from the deeps;
The flood foams gray; the whirling waters reel,
Now like its prey whereon at last it sweeps,
The ocean swallows up the vessel's keel.
The billows rage—exult, oh soul of mine,
Soon shalt thou enter the Lord's sacred shrine !

III.

TO THE WEST WIND.

Oh West, how fragrant breathes thy gentle air,
Spikenard and aloes on thy pinions glide.
Thou blow'st from spicy chambers, not from there
Where angry winds and tempests fierce abide.
As on a bird's wings thou dost waft me home,
Sweet as a bundle of rich myrrh to me.
And after thee yearn all the throngs that roam
And furrow with light keel the rolling sea.
Desert her not—our ship—bide with her oft,
When the day sinks and in the morning light.
Smooth thou the deeps and make the billows soft,
Nor rest save at our goal, the sacred height.
Chide thou the East that chafes the raging flood,
And swells the towering surges wild and rude.
What can I do, the elements' poor slave?
Now do they hold me fast, now leave me free;
Cling to the Lord, my soul, for He will save,
Who caused the mountains and the winds to be.

III.

MOSES BEN ESRA.

(ABOUT 1100.)

EXTRACTS FROM THE BOOK OF TARSHISH, OR
"NECKLACE OF PEARLS."

I.

The shadow of the houses leave behind,
In the cool boscage of the grove reclined
The wine of friendship from love's goblet drink,
And entertain with cheerful speech the mind.

Drink, friend! behold, the dreary winter's gone,
The mantle of old age has time withdrawn.
The sunbeam glitters in the morning dew,
O'er hill and vale youth's bloom is surging on.

Cup-bearer! quench with snow the goblet's fire,
Even as the wise man cools and stills his ire.
Look, when the jar is drained, upon the brim
The light foam melteth with the heart's desire.

Cup-bearer! bring anear the silver bowl,
And with the glowing gold fulfil the whole,
Unto the weak new vigor it imparts,
And without lance subdues the hero's soul.

My love sways, dancing, like the myrtle-tree,
The masses of her curls disheveled, see !
She kills me with her darts, intoxicates
My burning blood, and will not set me free.

Within the aromatic garden come.
And slowly in its shadows let us roam,
The foliage be the turban for our brows,
And the green branches o'er our heads a dome.

All pain thou with the goblet shalt assuage,
The wine-cup heals the sharpest pangs that rage,
Let others crave inheritance of wealth,
Joy be our portion and our heritage.

Drink in the garden, friend, anigh the rose,
Richer than spice's breath the soft air blows.
If it should cease a little traitor then,
A zephyr light its secret would disclose.

II.

Thou who art clothed in silk, who drawest on
Proudly thy raiment of fine linen spun,
Bethink thee of the day when thou alone
Shalt dwell at last beneath the marble stone.

Anigh the nests of adders thine abode,
With the earth-crawling serpent and the toad.
Trust in the Lord, He will sustain thee there,
And without fear thy soul shall rest with God.

If the world flatter thee with soft-voiced art,
Know ' tis a cunning witch who charms thy heart,
Whose habit is to wed man's soul with grief,
And those who are close-bound in love to part.

He who bestows his wealth upon the poor,
Has only lent it to the Lord, be sure—
Of what avail to clasp it with clenched hand ?
It goes not with us to the grave obscure.

The voice of those who dwell within the tomb,
Who in corruption's house have made their home ;
"Oh ye who wander o'er us still to-day,
When will ye come to share with us the gloom ?"

How can'st thou ever of the world complain,
And murmuring, burden it with all thy pain ?
Silence ! thou art a traveler at an inn,
A guest, who may but over night remain.

Be thou not wroth against the proud, but show
How he who yesterday great joy did know,
To-day is begging for his very bread,
And painfully upon a crutch must go.

How foolish they whose faith is fixed upon
The treasures of their worldly wealth alone,
Far wiser were it to obey the Lord,
And only say, " the will of God be done ! "

Has Fortune smiled on thee? Oh do not trust
Her reckless joy, she still deceives and must.
Perpetual snares she spreads about thy feet,
Thou shalt not rest till thou art mixed with dust.

Man is a weaver on the earth, ' tis said,
Who weaves and weaves—his own days are the thread,
And when the length allotted he hath spun,
All life is over and all hope is dead.

IN THE NIGHT.

Unto the house of prayer my spirit yearns,
Unto the sources of her being turns,
To where the sacred light of heaven burns,
She struggles thitherward by day and night.

The splendor of God's glory blinds her eyes,
Up without wings she soareth to the skies,
With silent aspiration seeks to rise,
In dusky evening and in darksome night.

To her the wonders of God's works appear,
She longs with fervor Him to draw anear,
The tidings of His glory reach her ear,
From morn to even, and from night to night.

The banner of thy grace did o'er me rest,
Yet was thy worship banished from my breast.
Almighty, thou didst seek me out and test
To try and to instruct me in the night.

I dare not idly on my pillow lie,
With winged feet to the shrine I fain would fly,
When chained by leaden slumbers heavily,
Men rest in imaged shadows, dreams of night.

Infatuate I trifled youth away,
In nothingness dreamed through my manhood's day.
Therefore my streaming tears I may not stay,
They are my meat and drink by day and night.

In flesh imprisoned is the son of light,
This life is but a bridge when seen aright.
Rise in the silent hour and pray with might,
Awake and call upon thy God by night!

Hasten to cleanse thyself of sin, arise!
Follow Truth's path that leads unto the skies,
As swift as yesterday existence flies,
Brief even as a watch within the night.

Man enters life for trouble; all he has,
And all that he beholds, is pain, alas!
Like to a flower does he bloom and pass,
He fadeth like a vision of the night.

The surging floods of life around him roar,
Death feeds upon him, pity is no more
To others all his riches he gives o'er,
And dieth in the middle hour of night.

Crushed by the burden of my sins I pray,
Oh, wherefore shunned I not the evil way?
Deep are my sighs, I weep the livelong day,
And wet my couch with tears night after night.

My spirit stirs, my streaming tears still run,
Like to the wild birds' notes my sorrows' tone,
In the hushed silence loud resounds my groan,
My soul arises moaning in the night.

Within her narrow cell oppressed with dread,
Bare of adornment and with grief bowed head
Lamenting, many a tear her sad eyes shed,
She weeps with anguish in the gloomy night.

For tears my burden seem to lighten best,
Could I but weep my heart's blood, I might rest.
My spirit bows with mighty grief oppressed,
I utter forth my prayer within the night.

Youth's charm has like a fleeting shadow gone,
With eagle wings the hours of life have flown.
Alas! the time when pleasure I have known,
I may not now recall by day or night.

The haughty scorn pursues me of my foe,
Evil his thought, yet soft his speech and low.
Forget it not, but bear his purpose so
Forever in thy mind by day and night.

Observe a pious fast, be whole again,
Hasten to purge thy heart of every stain.
No more from prayer and penitence refrain,
But turn unto thy God by day and night.

He speaks : " My son, yea, I will send thee aid,
Bend thou thy steps to me, be not afraid.
No nearer friend than I am, hast thou made,
Possess thy soul in patience one more night."

FROM THE "DIVAN."

My thoughts impelled me to the resting-place
Where sleep my parents, many a friend and brother.
I asked them (no one heard and none replied):
" Do ye forsake me, too, oh father, mother ? "
Then from the grave, without a tongue, these cried,
And showed my own place waiting by their side

LOVE SONG OF ALCHARISI.

I.

The long-closed door, oh open it again, send me back
    once more my fawn that had fled.
On the day of our reunion, thou shalt rest by my side,
    there wilt thou shed over me the streams of thy
    delicious perfume.
Oh beautiful bride, what is the form of thy friend, that
    thou say to me, Release him, send him away ?
He is the beautiful-eyed one of ruddy glorious aspect—
    that is my friend, him do thou detain.

II.

Hail to thee, Son of my friend, the ruddy, the bright
    colored one ! Hail to thee whose temples are like
    a pomegranate.
Hasten to the refuge of thy sister, and protect the son
    of Isaiah against the troops of the Ammonites.
What art thou, O Beauty, that thou shouldst inspire
    love ? that thy voice should ring like the voices of
    the bells upon the priestly garments ?
The hour wherein thou desirest my love, I shall hasten
    to meet thee. Softly will I drop beside thee like
    the dew upon Hermon.

THE END.

Songs of a Semite:
THE DANCE TO DEATH,
AND OTHER POEMS,
— BY —
EMMA LAZARUS,
AUTHOR OF "ADMETUS, AND OTHER POEMS," " ALIDE," "TRANSLATIONS
FROM HEINE," ETC.

Price, in paper .   .   .   .   86 PAGES, 8vo. .   .   .   .   Twenty-five cents.
"   " Cloth .   .   .   . Fifty   "

This volume contains "The Dance to Death" (a tragedy in five acts), and other poems which have recently appeared in THE AMERICAN HEBREW, as well as several Judaic poems by this gifted author which have not, hitherto, been presented in permanent form, and will include a number of Translations from the mediæval Spanish-Hebrew Poets—Gabirol, Ha Levi and Ben Esra; an In Memoriam on the death of Rev. J. J. Lyons, The Banner of the Jew, in Exile, Crowing of the Red Cock, The Guardian of the Red Disk, and her latest poem, "The New Year", written for the Rosh Hashanah (New Year) number of THE AMERICAN HEBREW.

The volume is printed on fine, tinted paper, from large, clear type.

As the edition is limited, early application for copies should be made.

Dealers, to whom liberal discount will be given, can be supplied through the News Companies or by the publishers,   THE AMERICAN HEBREW,

(Telephone Address: 39th, 243)   498-500 Third Avenue, New York.

☞Sent, postpaid, on receipt of price.

NOTICES OF THE PRESS.

ADMETUS, AND OTHER POEMS.

" We give a hearty welcome to Miss Lazarus. Her book has been a thorough surprise. We took it up with the greatest diffidence, especially when we saw that the first poem was ' Admetus.' Admirers of Browning will, we know, think we are uttering something akin to blasphemy, when we say that the ' Admetus ' of Miss Lazarus will in some points bear comparison with ' Balaustion's Adventure'. . . . . We cannot help saying that we have not for a long time seen any volume of poetry which in so many various ways gives such promise as the present."—*Westminster Review.*

" The volume by Miss Lazarus is full of good things. . . . . . The chief poems are all good. She is able to produce vivid effect without display of force. Her subtlety is marked, and she leaves no traces of her art. There is something—and not much—wanting to complete her success and place her alongside of the masters."—*London Athenaeum.*

"' Admetus ' is a fine poem. We catch now and then a Tennysonian echo in the verse, but there are no feeble lines, and passages both of description and dialogue are full of energy. Emma Lazarus is a new name to us in American poetry, but ' Admetus ' is not the work of a ' prentice-hand.' "—*New York Evening Post.*

" Few recent volumes of verse compare favora-

bly with the spirited and musical expression of these genuine effusions of Emma Lazarus."— HENRY T. TUCKERMAN, in *The Boston Transcript.*

" Miss Lazarus must be hailed by impartial literary criticism as a poet of rare original power. She has unconsciously caught from admiring perusal more perhaps of the style of Tennyson's ' Arthurian Idylls ' in her narrative and dramatic pieces than would seem fitly to attend the perfectly fresh and independent stream of her thought. The tone, the phrases, the turns of melody in her blank verse lines too, often remind us of the English master whom she follows in the craft of rhythmic diction. But her conceptions of each theme, and the whole compass of her ideas and emotions differ essentially from those of preceding or contemporary masters. In her treatment of the story of ' Alcestis ' and ' Admetus,' one of the two Greek subjects among the poems of this volume, she is far happier than Mr. Browning in his half adaption of ' Euripides.' . . . . . The conflict between Hercules and Death, and the return to life of Alcestis, are represented with more force as well as grace in this poem than in that of Mr. Browning. . . . . . . It will be no surprise to us, after the present volume, if she hereafter take a high place among the best poets in this age of our common English tongue "--*Illustrated London News.*

ALIDE; AN EPISODE OF GOETHE'S LIFE.

" Alide is a sad story, but told in a very charming way. Miss Lazarus has strength, grace and simplicity of style, and treats with equal skill both the outer and inner life of her characters."—*Boston Advertiser.*

Miss Lazarus, if not the best of our living poet-

esses, is among the best, and she shows herself in this volume, a mistress also of prose. With these claims to recognition as a writer, she has also a claim to be recognized as a very gifted student and illustrator of the great genius of the age."—*Philadelphia Bulletin.*

TRANSLATIONS FROM HEINE.

" . . . . Let us none the less do justice to Miss Lazarus. She is terse, sparing of words, direct, has a keen musical ear, and a good command of language. To have the tenderness, the pathos, the mystery, the despair, the pictorial acuteness, the strength of Heine is much, and these Miss Lazarus can fairly command."—*N. Y. Herald.*

" Miss Lazarus' version is a copy of an artist's work made by an artist's hand. The translator

is in sympathy with the author's most subtle thoughts and fancies.—*Th Critic.*

"   The renderings from the original are remarkably close, and enjoy the same freedom from involution or straining after effect that makes most of Heine's works limpid and places some of it at the very front of German literature."—*Century Magazine.*

THE AMERICAN HEBREW,

—⊹PUBLISHED EVERY FRIDAY.⊹—

498-500 Third Avenue, N. Y.

Terms, $3.00 per Annum. | Sample Copies, Free.

THE AMERICAN HEBREW

Is edited by a Board of Editors representing various phases of Judaism, and is therefore an independent and impartial Journal.

THE AMERICAN HEBREW

Has an abler staff of writers than any other American Jewish journal.

THE AMERICAN HEBREW

Is the leading American Jewish journal, and has come to be considered as such by its tone, its fairness, and the ability with which it is conducted.

Address,

THE AMERICAN HEBREW,

Telephone Address :—39th, 243.   498-500 Third Avenue.

THE ANCIENT RABBI AND THE MODERN MINISTER.

BY HON. MORITZ ELLINGER.

This paper was acknowledged to be the best article read at the last meeting of the "Rabbinical Literary Association". It was published in the columns of THE AMERICAN HEBREW, and the interest manifested in it led to its republication in convenient form.

24 PP.; PRICE, 15 CENTS.

Liberal Discount to the Trade.

☞ Sent Postpaid on receipt of Price. ☜

THE AMERICAN HEBREW,

Telephone Address :—39th, 243.   498-500 Third Avenue.